Razi Crossing ©

A True Story

Tom Burchill

Dedication

This book is dedicated to American diplomat Michael Metrinko who was instrumental in saving my brother's life and the lives of nine other people in Tabriz, Iran, February 1979. Even after the harrowing incident at the Tabriz consulate, Mr. Metrinko bravely continued his service in Iran, only to later become one of the 52 American hostages who endured 444 terrible days at the hands of their captors during the Tehran embassy takeover. To this day, Mr. Metrinko continues his tireless and dedicated service to the United States. As of this writing, he is serving in Cheghcheran in the remote Afghan province of Ghor.

Acknowledgements

I wish to acknowledge the following people for their direct and indirect contribution to the completion of this book: My brother, John Burchill, for going through the harrowing experiences described in this book and living to tell about it. American Consul, Michael Metrinko, for saving my brother's life and getting him home safely. Author and friend, Glenn J. Morgan, for providing valuable feedback and guidance on realizing my dream of seeing "Razi Crossing" published. Bookstore owner and author, Clyde Holloway, who inspired me to finish "Razi Crossing" by publishing his own poignant story of his father's experiences in World War Two. My neighbor and friend, Bob Knauer, who generously donated his time to provide me with valuable feedback before going to press. Finally, my wonderful wife, Jeannie, for proofing the manuscript, and for the many invaluable words of encouragement and support I needed to see this project through.

Preface

When my brother returned safely home from Iran in February 1979, our family was greatly relieved that he had returned to us against all odds. Physically, he was almost unrecognizable; sixty pounds lighter, gaunt and his skin darker by a half dozen shades. The difficult experience had taught John a few valuable life lessons. As we learned the full details of his amazing journey to Iran and back, I felt his story merited a wider telling and I urged him to write about it. But John was never one to seek publicity for himself, so he never bothered to go to the press or even write down his experiences. Mainly, he chose to share his story verbally among his family and friends. Despite my repeated prodding, I could never get him to take his story to the pen.

Three years later, John came back to the U.S. for a short visit home. By then our family had moved back to the U.S. Though the story idea still stewed in my head, John was not a step closer to writing of his experiences. I decided then that I should take the initiative to get things rolling. I wanted the events of his story to be documented while his memories were still fresh so I finally sat him down and recorded his experiences onto audio tape. When the interview was complete, I was excited about chronicling the story for some sort of publication. Perhaps I would write a magazine article, maybe a book or even a movie script. The story was full of promise, and I was full of good intentions.

Soon the months became years and nothing much became of my good intentions. Several times out of a sense of guilt, I made half-hearted attempts to start writing, but I never seemed to get past the first few pages. I quickly realized that there was a great chasm between knowing a great story well and telling it as a compelling and coherent piece of writing. Repeatedly, the story would come together in bits and pieces and then become disjointed again. At times, I wondered if I had in me what it would take to accomplish the task. Finally in frustration, I shamefully relented to the "someday I'll..." syndrome. The cassette tapes then sat idle in the back of my desk drawer for the next twenty years.

I had always believed that John's amazing story was worth telling to the world but before I knew it, the years had gotten away from us much too quickly. We had both become middle-aged men in our mid-forties. Then, the Iranians celebrated their 25th anniversary of the revolution. This was my wakeup call; a quarter century had slipped away and I had run out of excuses. That "someday" had finally arrived and I resolved that I had to get busy writing or admit to myself that I wasn't ever going to do it. I finally dusted off those old cassette tapes and started to listen to a familiar, but amazing tale. This is John's story.

Chapter 1
Echoes of a Distant Revolution

As of this writing, slightly more than twenty five years have already passed since the Iranian revolution of 1979. The massive geopolitical rift that was created by that event still echoes through the years as the animosity and hateful rhetoric between Washington and Tehran still continues unabated. That fateful year of 1979 was arguably a nadir in post-war WW-II American history. Our nation was already in a stupor reeling from aftermath of Vietnam, Watergate and the Middle East oil crisis. The once robust American economy was seemingly in an endless economic malaise that gripped the nation. Much of America's industrial heartland was rapidly becoming a rust-belt while it seemed the Japanese were destined to buy up what was left of America. On top of that, the incomes of ordinary people were being devoured by raging double digit inflation. Such were the downbeat sentiment of the times that many people had begun to believe that America's best days were behind us forever.

In that hour of weakness and self-doubt, America suffered another terrible blow from half a world away in Iran. To add insult to injury, on November 4th, 1979, a group of radical Islamist students seized the American embassy and members of its staff. Ultimately,

52 Americans were taken hostage; their blindfolded faces, jeered by hateful crowds became the symbol of American impotence for 444 long and difficult days. In an act of desperation to save our national pride, our once vaunted military mounted a heroic rescue attempt but that too went horribly wrong and cost the lives of eight more brave Americans. That day, American prestige had sunk to a new low.

To most Americans, the embassy hostage taking and its aftermath is the singular enduring memory of the Iranian crisis. Like the immortal images of D-day and Iwo Jima, these were the seminal events of the era that were burned into our collective psyche. A handful of powerful images propagated into our homes became the defining symbols of a great event that affected the lives of millions.

A full nine months prior to the hostage crisis in Tehran, another little publicized crisis occurred when the American consulate in the northwestern city of Tabriz was stormed by Islamic revolutionaries. Among the ten people taken from the consulate at gunpoint that day, was my brother, John Burchill. It was by a sheer fluke that my brother had found himself immersed in the center of that distant revolution. He was just a wayward college dropout seeking a little adventure and fun in the Middle East. In fact he had only expected to stay in Iran for less than two weeks.

In the course of his youthful adventures during the previous summer, John had run afoul of Iranian law and landed himself in prison at Tabriz. Our family was stunned to hear of his incarceration in Iran, but we had to accept the fact that John had brought it upon himself. He had made a series of bad life decisions which ultimately lead to misadventure and misfortune. My parents did what they could, hoping to somehow secure a lighter sentence and an early release for John, but we honestly expected that it would be at least several years before we saw him as a free man again.

****

Our family knew that John was strong-willed and he would survive his imprisonment. As the months passed however, the issue of incarceration became less of a concern to us. In the larger scheme of things, there were much more ominous developments that were engulfing in Iran. By the end of 1978, it became clear that John had landed himself in the wrong place at the wrong time as the Shah's government stood on increasingly shaky ground.

That winter, we watched the events unfolding from our home in Germany. We remember well the rage and hatred for America that we witnessed each night on our television screens. We could only watch in quiet agony as each day brought more bad news of riots and unchecked anti-government violence across Iran. As civil order collapsed in Iran and the revolution ignited in its full fury, we could only stand by and watch helplessly.

Soon, all communications to the consulates were cut off and we feared it would be just a matter of time before some angry mob vented their rage on my brother. Things had gone so awry in that country that we could no longer imagine any means by which John could come out of this predicament unscathed. We knew that it would take nothing short of a miracle to bring John back home safe.

We wondered how it could have all come to this. Why had fate so cruelly woven together a series of unfortunate events that conspired to entrap my brother and serve him up as fodder for some lousy revolution? The irony of my brother's unintentionally wandering onto center stage amidst millions of angry Iranians thirsting for American blood was too much to bear.

Against such odds, our family quietly and stoically prayed for that miracle to happen. The rest was in the hands of fate and we could do nothing more. John had never cared much for matters of faith, but it must be true that God looks after the wretched. For in the end, John was granted not one, but a series of miracles that finally brought him home safe and unscathed.

Chapter 2
A Wild One and a Wandering Clan

My brother John was born the eldest of the three Burchill boys. From the very get-go, he was always the loud and rambunctious one. Fearless to a fault, he was endlessly getting himself into trouble or creating mayhem of one sort or another. My poor mother used to dread going to Johnny's parent-teacher conferences. Being quite the polite and proper Japanese lady, his wild antics at school were a source of continual embarrassment for her. Young Johnny was a real handful and gleefully got into trouble on a regular basis. He was smart, athletic and rough around the edges, but he was never a "bad" kid. Johnny always had a good heart, but his propensity for wild behavior always got the best of him. It was not altogether surprising that his childhood traits would only preface what was to come later in life. Even in his middle age, the wisdom gained from life often still takes a back seat to an occasional brush with the wild side. That's our Johnny.

By contrast, I was always the quiet and studious one of the family. Only a year and a half younger, I was not nearly as trouble prone as John, but then again, I concocted my own share of trouble in a quiet and calculated way. Mom always knew when John was making trouble, but she rightly worried about me most when

I had been too quiet! When I wasn't busy cooking up my own shenanigans, there was always Johnny to entice me into his next round of mischief.

Finally, the youngest of us, Roger came along eight years later. Sweet and gentle, Roger has been the baby of the family.

****

From the beginning, fate would have it that we would become a well-traveled family. In the mid 1950's our dad, Jim, had gone to Japan as a young Navy seaman. While he was there, he met and fell in love with Miki, the woman who would later become our mother. It was a typical postwar romance of a young serviceman abroad finding adventure and love. It was a story as natural and old as history itself.

Unfortunately, when the news of this relationship reached the ears of Jim's mother, Mildred, she was incensed. Perhaps, the memories of the war against Japan were still too fresh for her to stomach the thought of her son cavorting with the recent enemy. Perhaps she felt it was an affront to her late husband, John L. Burchill who had served aboard the destroyer U.S.S. Nicholas during the war. In fact it was the crew of the U.S.S. Nicholas that had the honor of transporting representatives of the allied powers to the U.S.S. Missouri to accept the formal Japanese surrender in Tokyo bay.

Mother Mildred had wasted no time in contacting her senator to have her son immediately reassigned to the U.S. In a heartbeat, dad found himself on a ship headed back to the U.S. Before he left, dad swore to Miki that he would somehow return for her. Thousands of young servicemen in those days made similar vows to their sweethearts they left behind overseas, but the reality was that few such promises were ever kept. As Jim reluctantly set sail for the U.S., he was unaware that Miki was already pregnant with Johnny.

A few weeks later, dad reported to his final duty station in Bangor, Maine. Mother Mildred had made sure that Jim would be as far from Japan as possible while serving stateside. Disappointed but undaunted, dad served out his obligation to the Navy and received his honorable discharge. Finally, he was a free man again. With little more than a duffle bag on his shoulder and a small amount of money he had managed to save during the past few months, Jim knew without a doubt what he would do next. He walked out of the naval base and headed straight for Japan, 7,000 miles away.

****

So it would come to pass that dad would spend the next 17 years in Japan. He eventually made a life long career as a civil servant working for the Army & Air Force Exchange service (AAFES). AAFES primarily operated the Base and Post Exchanges, but they also ran the barber shops, snack bars, dry cleaners, movie theaters, etc. Dad's job was to make sure all the movie theaters in his region got their films on time and everything ran smoothly in his territory. A fringe benefit of his job was that on weekends we got to see a lot of free movies. In the days before there were such things as video rental stores and VCRs, it was quite something to have private access to a library of hundreds of current movies. All of our friends that we invited down to the office screening room thought we were just too cool!

Where ever in the world the U.S. military needed motion picture entertainment, my dad went and we followed. In addition to our many years in Japan, dad's assignments took him to Thailand, Vietnam, Germany, and several cities within the U.S. For all intents and purposes, we grew up as civilian versions of military brats, always living on or near military bases across the globe. During those 20 years on the move across several continents, we never had the time to set down our roots like most folks. But every few years, life offered us a whole new adventure.

In the summer of 1975, we were living in St. Louis, Missouri. We had already been back in the U.S. for two years and we were all were itching to go back overseas again. After our last assignment in beautiful and exotic Thailand, the stateside assignments were just too sedate. Life just didn't measure up on the adventure scale. The wanderlust just seemed to be in our blood, and we yearned again for new cultures and new experiences. Late that summer, our prayers were finally answered. Dad received orders to relocate to Bad Nauheim, Germany and we were off to explore Europe.

****

When we arrived in Germany in that fall, I was sixteen years old, John was just short of turning eighteen and little Roger was eight. As soon as we had settled into our new home in Nieder Weisel, I headed off to start my junior year of High School at Frankfurt am Main. John on the other hand, wasn't quite sure what he wanted to do. He had graduated from high school a few months earlier, so he was looking forward to some time out to explore his options for the future.

John had always been a prolific reader, so he basically took a year off for a literary sabbatical of sorts. Aside from his extensive reading, John's primary function during the day was to chauffeur my mom around town. Mom never learned to drive so his presence came in handy for those quick trips to the commissary and PX. He chipped in here and there with some household chores, but in truth, John was rapidly becoming a man of leisure. Life was mainly about just goofing off and having fun.

John was becoming every parent's nightmare; the grown up kid that wouldn't leave home. Despite some heart-to-heart discussions regarding a number of possible options, John seemed not to have any real direction or ambition in his life. He was indecisive and kept putting off making any kind of major commitment. After nearly ten months of foot-dragging, my folk's patience was wearing real thin. John's days of freeloading were about to come to an end.

That day came when dad finally laid down the law; either go back to school or get a job. John couldn't dodge the issue any more; the message was loud and clear. He would get the boot one way or another. Seeking the path of least resistance, John opted to go to college. Echoing the long-ago sentiments of Claire Swan, John chose to enroll at the University of Maryland's Munich campus. He really enjoyed living in Germany and wished to stay in Europe. That fall of 1976, John headed south to Munich for a taste of the college life.

Chapter 3
Munich Campus

On the outskirts of the city of Munich, there is an old American Army base formerly known as McGraw Kaserne. The Kaserne was occupied by the U.S. Army at the end of World War II and primarily served the Army's administrative needs in the Southern Bavaria region for the better part of fifty years. With the end of the Cold War however, the Kaserne's useful days came to an end and closed for good in 1993. After the Americans vacated the premises, the Kaserne reverted back to the German government and shortly after, the German Police moved in as the new occupants of the Kaserne.

The old Kaserne is dominated by a large brownstone building that was once the AAFES headquarters for Europe. Of particular interest to this story though, is another sizeable building that stands across the Kaserne. Known simply as building 2, this white-washed building was built in 1945 and stood five-stories tall. Today the structure serves as the German Police Cadet training school. Prior to the arrival of the German Police cadets however, this otherwise non-descript building had a distinguished, and rather uncommon post-war history. For a period of forty two years, from 1950 to 1992, this building served as home to the European campus of the

University of Maryland. While glamorous in name and located in an exotic and exciting foreign city, the campus was anything but.

****

The Munich campus building was most Spartan in its appearance as well as its facilities. The university was unceremoniously located above the U.S. Army Commissary - and for a time, the movie theater as well. It was a most unlikely college campus in so many ways, but it was a real university with many a distinguished faculty for its small size. It had many shortcomings, but to those of us who were once students there, we remember it as a very special place that offered a unique and rewarding educational and cultural experience.

What made it all work was that Munich itself was such a world-class city. Munich offered a broad range of attractions including museums, theaters, historic palaces, parks and cathedrals. There was always plenty to explore and experience around this great town. The excellent regional rail system also allowed quick and easy access to the outlying Bavarian lakes and nearby historic towns. Best of all, by a rather fortunate fate of geography, Munich was located in almost the exact geographic center of Europe. This convenient locale provided the students with access to a wide range of travel and cultural activities not readily available to their stateside counterparts. Weekend forays to Austria, Switzerland and Italy were commonplace activities. The winter and spring breaks meant opportunities for longer trips to France, England, Spain, Greece, and Czechoslovakia. Even destinations such as Egypt, Turkey and Israel were there for those who could afford it.

Despite its foreign locale and quirky character, the Munich Campus was in so many ways a reflection of its bigger stateside cousin in College Park, Maryland. As in any other American university, the daily lives of the students revolved around academics, campus social events and a range of extracurricular activities. Although the facilities and sports programs were limited as compared to large stateside universities, the Munich Terrapins gave the school its mascot and a team to cheer on. The Munich campus was an opportunity to experience the best of both worlds.

****

To understand how this quirky campus abroad came into existence, we first need to digress back to post-war Germany of 1948. Back then many areas of Munich still showed the scars of war from the allied bombing raids during World War II. There was also a certain lingering distrust of the German populace as it was so recently that the Germans and Americans were mercilessly killing each other in combat. There were still too many fresh reminders of the just ended Nazi era. One only needed to visit the nearby town of Dachau to witness first hand what horrors took place there. As one of the first concentration camps, the camp at Dachau was the harbinger of things to come. Though it had been just three years since the ovens went cold, the stench of death would linger in the memories of the townsfolk for years to come. World history had just endured a most brutal and pivotal inflection point and another was about to begin in a city further north called Berlin. But in this most unlikely setting, a determined young daughter of a U.S. Army Colonel would stir up her own little piece of Cold war history in Europe.

In 1948, Claire Swan was in her senior year of high school in Munich. During her time there, Claire experienced a side of Germany and the Bavarian culture that resonated positively with her. She saw past the perversions of Nazism as an aberration of history and came to develop a deep appreciation of the Bavarian people, their culture and their rich history. She had adopted Munich as her home town and desperately wanted to stay on in Germany.

Her father, Colonel Swan, was also the commanding officer of the Kaserne. He had other ideas about his daughter's future. Like everyone else, he fully expected that his daughter would return to the U.S. that fall to start on her university education. In spite of her father's wishes, Claire believed that there were so many more students with similar sentiments about wanting to spend their college years in Europe. The solution to her dilemma was simple; she would convince an accredited American university to open a satellite campus right there in Munich! Such a university could provide the dependents of military personnel a chance to attend an accredited American University while living in one of Europe's great cities. It was perfect!

With the charismatic innocence of youth, Claire began a determined lobbying campaign starting with her own father. Impressed by his daughter's intense devotion to the cause, her father finally gave in and threw all his power and support behind his daughter. Expensive and novel ideas are not easily bought into by the military establishment - especially those dreamed up by some eighteen year old girl. Even as the Berlin crisis exploded and raised the specter of a new conflict on the continent, Claire pressed forward in her quest. Finally, in the fall of 1950 Claire's dream became a reality and the European Campus of the University of Maryland opened its doors for the first time.

The new European campus was an immediate success and over the ensuing decades it continued to grow and evolve, adding students, faculty and new programs. During its forty-two years of service, many tens of thousands of military dependents received their first two years of university education here before going on to State-side universities to complete their undergraduate degrees. Thirty years later, the cold war was still red hot and glasnost was unheard of, but this unique campus in this magnificent city, was enjoying its heyday with over 1,500 registered students.

Chapter 4
Temptations and Rabble Rousing

Since his arrival in Munich, John had discovered a renewed sense of purpose and vigor to his life. Exploring the exciting new city, coupled with the academic challenges of the university environment seemed to bring out the best of him. During his first semester at school, John did very well in his studies. He showed genuine interest in many of his courses and produced some good grades in the process. My parents were mightily relieved to see him doing so well and moving on with his life. Overall, things seemed to be coming together pretty well for John.

The experience of going away to attend college is a significant stepping stone in the life of a student. For most young adults, it is their first real experience of living away from their families and being on their own. It is also a time of new found freedoms and fun that needs to be tempered with measured responsibilities. You learn to make all of your own choices and you prioritize your life between fun and obligations. It is a time when individuals either grow up and stay focused on their responsibilities and goals, or else they fall victim to impulse and temptations.

Despite his promising start at Munich, it wasn't long before John was seduced by the siren's song of the campus party crowd; the wild keg parties. For all of John's inherent abilities and potential, he was born with an Achilles' heal that has led to constant distractions and detours throughout his life. John took after his dad and had a rather innate affinity for drinking and revelry. Dad always maintained that it was the Irish blood that was mostly to blame. Unlike the students who did well to balance their studies with the occasional indulgence, John's very nature was such that he found it difficult to temper himself in these matters. So it didn't take long before John came to embrace the campus die-hard "party animals" as his inner circle of friends. Not surprisingly, his "friends" were a pretty motley bunch of campus misfits who shared a single-minded devotion to partying hard, and partying often. After he had been adopted into this unruly crowd, John quickly rose to prominence and became notorious around campus for his boisterous excesses and beer swilling exploits.

Initially, dad had looked upon John's wild activities and drinking as little more than frat house pranks and blowing off the steam of youthful exuberance. Of course, dad didn't have a whole lot of credibility himself when it came to lecturing John about drinking to excess either. Over the years, dad earned himself quite a reputation as a hard-drinking party animal. As long as John brought home reasonably good grades and stayed out of major trouble, dad was willing to look the other way with a wink and a nudge. Of course mom wasn't nearly as tolerant about John's excessive drinking. She had seen it all before and she knew it was too much a case of "like father, like son". Unfortunately, about all she could do was to tell John to cool it and hope it resonated with him at some point before things got too out of control.

****

By the time John returned to school for the start of his

second year, he was already well beyond the point of no return. His academic life was starting to slide downhill; his grades began to plummet and he frequently shunned his school obligations. Just about everything in John's life was being eclipsed by his need to drink and party. Deep down inside, he knew he was hanging with the wrong crowd, but he couldn't help being drawn that way. The allure was too much for him to resist.

John even began to form a rather convoluted rationale to justify his incessant partying. Together with his number one party sidekick, Pat Tiahrt, they both brashly came to see themselves as the keepers of the school legacy. They felt it was their solemn duty to boldly uphold the campus' reputation as "the greatest party school on the planet." Whether it was true or not, in their often hung-over minds, this became a perfectly rational charter and a noble pursuit to which they could devote their lives.

John and Pat also conjured up other creative ways to morph their beer swilling habits into a kind of a pseudo-academic cultural study tour of Bavaria. Their regular forays to the Hofbrau Haus and other legendary beer halls of Munich were their own special way of examining and appreciating the "essence" of Bavarian culture first hand. They eagerly memorized classic beer hall toasts as well as the lyrics to numerous "oompah" beer drinking songs. After all, they reasoned, it was a well known fact that for two raucous weeks each year, Munich played host to the world-renowned Oktoberfest – the undisputed mother of all keg parties. Munich also happened to be home to some half-dozen of the largest beer halls in the world, some able to serve up to four thousand partygoers at a time. And just to make sure that the good times kept on rolling in Munich, there were several other beer fests that took place throughout the year. No doubt then, that good beer and hearty partying was a truly important aspect of Munich's cultural heritage and life. With such a heady reputation at stake, one could empathize just how John and his pals came to take to partying with such zeal. Their logic may have been convoluted as hell, but to John and Pat, partying was much more than a mere diversion; it was now their mission.

No one who has ever attended the Munich Campus would deny that it was a hard partying school. According to campus lore, it was said that Playboy Magazine wanted to rank the University of Maryland's Munich campus as Playboy's "#1 ranked party school" that year. However, because it was not located within the continental United States, they were summarily disqualified for this dubious honor. Their moment of glory stolen, the honor went to Notre Dame for that year. This tragic news was received with great disappointment by John and his pals. Accordingly, they agreed that they should collectively drown their sorrows with more beer.

Over the course of his second year at school, John's life became inextricably entwined with the hard-core party crowd. As he was one to believe that there was no such thing as having too much fun, he regularly carried it to the extremes. With his genetic disposition came both the stamina and the stomach for consuming prodigious amounts of alcohol. John could just about drink anyone under the table – and like the Energizer Bunny, still keep going and going. This was all very lamentable because John was otherwise a pretty darn smart guy. He had always been a prolific reader and well versed in a wide range of subjects, particularly world history and politics. In fact I remember the time when he read all 1,063 pages of Ayn Rand's "Atlas Shrugged" in just three days! When sober, John could be an engaging conversationalist as well as a very keen debater. Unfortunately, John's perennial problem was that without strong supervision and focus, he would often gravitate towards joining the wrong crowd. Consequently, he would end up doing some really dumb things - and dumb things he did!

****

John and his pals were notorious around the campus as a rebellious, raucous, and totally irreverent bunch. They pretty much offended everyone in just about every way they could. Mostly it was all for the sport of taunting or pissing off other people. Much of what they did was boorish behavior at its worst. One of their particularly malicious stunts was to march through a German residential area late at night chanting an old Nazi rally slogan, "Auf unserem geliebten Fuerher, drei mal: Sieg Heil: sieg heil, sieg heil, sieg heil!" Their aim was to piss off the locals by rousing them awake with this offensive commotion in the middle of the night. They would keep it up until they had successfully elicited an angry "halts maul, du aschlohen!" (Shut your trap, you assholes!). Only then did they consider it "mission accomplished" and quickly melted away into the night laughing hysterically. It was obnoxious and it was stupid, but they found a certain obscene entertainment in it all.

Unfortunately, their appetite for stirring up trouble didn't end there. One night, they decided that "things were just too peaceful" so they decided to incite a riot at the school dorms. They started by going around the dorms banging on pots and pans while screaming "Riot! Riot"! Their intent was to start a general melee on campus and the group was quickly joined in by dozens of bored, like-minded students. To add to the din and the effect of growing mayhem, they threw beer bottles out the windows and sent them smashing onto the sidewalks below. They also ignited numerous butane-filled balloon bombs that lit up the night with spectacular balls of flame. To their perverse pleasure, the stunt seemed to be succeeding and taking on a life of its own.

As the commotion reached a fever pitch, the Military Police soon came out in full force to quell the disturbance. Even the college Dean, Mr. McMahon made a personal appearance to calm down the seemingly pointless uprising. No real serious damage had been done, but when the investigations were completed, John had earned a very special place on the Dean's list - the other kind of list, that is.

****

John's notoriety was assured its place in the annals of the Munich Campus. In fact, when I followed my brother's footsteps and entered U of M the following year, John's notorious legacy was immediately felt:

There I was, minding my own business on the first day of English 101. My professor was the wiry Dr. Heminway, a brilliant but often quirky fellow who had a knack for some real off-beat humor. He would often say things like "Mr. Smith, please come into my orifice after class, won't you?" Personally, I'm glad I never had to say answer that question myself! As Dr. Heminway went down the roll call, he welcomed each of the freshmen.

"Mr. Burchill, Thomas," Are you here?

I responded with a curt "here", expecting him to quickly move on down the list. Instead Dr. Heminway paused to scrutinize me for what seemed an uncomfortable length, drumming his finger on his chin. When he finally spoke, he said, "Mr. Burchill, you wouldn't happen to have had a brother that went here recently, did you?"

Suddenly, all eyes in the class were on me. Self-conscious, I squirmed in my seat and answered, "Uh, yes that's right".

"Would that be the INFAMOUS Mr. John Burchill?"

My first day at college, and I was already exposed as being related to the campus Mob! "Yes Sir, that's the one", I answered with a forced smile. I wasn't sure where all this was leading, but perhaps Dr. Heminway was wondering if he could expect similar trouble from me.

"Soooo you're John Burchill's younger brother, are you?" He teased his goatee and then muttered with a raised eyebrow. "You two… you're very different. Yessss, very different…."

****

And so it was, that by the beginning of spring semester of 1978, John had lost all motivation for his studies. His once promising college experience had deteriorated into a series of drinking binges followed by one stupid stunt after another. He was tired of school and life no longer offered anything to drive him. He was adrift in a long downward spiral. Both mentally and physically, he had completely dropped out of college. In fact he had not even bothered to attend a class for weeks. As the long summer break approached, John was bored, restless and had no clear plans for his future. This was his recipe for more trouble.

Chapter 5
A Day Late and a D-Mark Short

The weather had turned warmer and the arrival of summer break meant the majority of the dorm students would begin packing up to head home for the summer. The dorm students were almost all exclusively dependents of military personnel stationed abroad. The places they called their "homes" were located on or near the many military bases scattered throughout Germany, England and Italy – pretty much just about anywhere their parents happened to be stationed at the time. Some of the students even hailed from locations in North Africa and other parts of the Middle East. One was from as far away as Japan.

On that final weekend of the semester, the dorms were bustling with students and their parental units. In the parking lot, dozens of cars were loading up and many tearful hugs and goodbyes were heard as the departing students left to go on their separate ways. They would take with them the memories of strong friendships forged from sharing a unique and wonderful life experience. Most of the students were headed for home while some of the more fortunate ones embarked on their grand backpacking tour of Europe. Come the fall, most of these students would go on to stateside universities to complete their undergraduate degrees.

As this time honored ritual unfolded in the courtyard, both John and Pat were conspicuously absent from the scene.

That morning, John and Pat had drifted from dorm to dorm checking to see if anyone needed help with cleaning up their remaining beer supply. A few were sympathetic and they managed to score a couple of free beers, but most were less than accommodating. Some were down right hostile and rebuffed the mooching duo with a sharp "Fuck you, assholes!" Not to be outdone, John and Pat returned the raised middle finger along with a few other obscene gestures to boot.

Figuring that they had pretty much pushed their luck around the dorms, the two headed for the local canteen and reluctantly bought their own brews. John had a little extra money that week. Although the money was meant to pay for his train fare home, he wasn't planning on spending it for train tickets. He had other plans for the money. A week earlier, John had sent a letter home saying that he wouldn't be coming home at the end of the semester as planned. Instead, he had decided to stay in Munich and get a job for the summer. He would probably be coming home in the fall unless something more permanent turned up.

The news of John's staying on in Munich didn't exactly sit well with mom and dad. Unfortunately, John's dismal report card hadn't arrived home yet so my dad didn't have too much reason to be hard on him. On the other hand, mom could smell trouble brewing from afar – she knew John too well. Dad called John to talk him out of his decision, but John wasn't about to take "NO" for an answer. He was already twenty years old; he insisted that if he wanted to be on his own, he was old enough and dad couldn't legally stop him. Dad knew all too well that stubbornness was another trait that they both shared to their detriment. Dad decided there was no use arguing further and relented - with the caveat that John would come home if he didn't find a job within next two weeks.

****

Back in those days, our family lived in the quaint little farm village of Nieder Wiesel. Nieder Weisel was located in the picturesque Wetterau valley in the central German state of Hessen. Our little village was about four hundred kilometers northwest of Munich. Aside from a couple of small cities nearby, it was largely rural farmland and forested mountains. The nearest major city was Frankfurt am Main, fifty kilometers to the south. The Wetterau was a pretty area with the Taunus Mountain range located just to the west of us. To the east, we could see Meunzenberg castle sitting on a hill and overlooking the valley.

As a budding young photographer, I reveled in this idyllic pastoral landscape. I spent almost all of my free time hiking, biking and photographing the area. Even dad's office reflected the general charm of the area. His "office" was located in a quaint World War II era barracks tucked away in a beautiful secluded valley at the foot hills of the Taunus Mountains. Interestingly, this was the very same building that had served as Hitler's secret western front headquarters in the winter of 1944/45. It was from here that he directed the historic battle of the Bulge. By the time the allies found out about the location, Hitler had already returned to his eastern front headquarters in East Prussia. The allies tried bombing the site but unfortunately most of bombs missed and fell on the adjacent little town instead. Thus, the structure survived the war to later become the regional office for AAFES.

Aside from the often fickle weather, living in this lovely area suited me just fine, but John saw things quite differently. Compared to the exciting cosmopolitan atmosphere of Munich, Nieder Weisel and its rural surroundings was positively "Dullsville" for him. After nearly two years of living the carefree and exciting life in Munich, John wasn't ready to let the fun and partying come to an end. He considered a return to Nieder Weisel as a death sentence of sorts. He was determined to avoid returning there at all costs.

Of course there was also the distasteful thought of having to face his unhappy parents back home. Mom and Dad had endured considerable financial hardships to send him to school but his grades this semester were downright abysmal. The A's and B's of the previous year had deteriorated steadily into D's and F's. Chances were pretty darn good that mom and dad were going to shut off the money tap completely. That meant that John wouldn't be going back to Munich in the fall and more than likely, they would make him take some boring civilian job at the nearby Giessen Army depot. In his mind, going home was simply not an option. In spite of his meager remaining finances, John was determined more than ever to find a way to stay in Munich and continue enjoying the lifestyle he so desired.

******

Now that the dormitories had already closed for the summer, John and Pat had to move fast. With their worldly belongings on their backs, they set out on their quest to find some shelter. Their plan was to start hitting up on anyone and everyone they knew that might be willing to give them a break and put a roof over their heads. Money was extremely tight and they needed a place to crash. They were prepared to sleep in parks and under bridges for a time if needed. Once they landed a summer job and got a paycheck, they could find a room to rent somewhere. Until then, it was time for some serious sucking up.

They dropped in at all of their usual haunts including the nearby Blue Room, a local watering hole where John and Pat had often hung out to shoot the breeze with the locals. Serendipitously, they conveniently ran into Mike on that day. Mike was an American ex-patriot who had decided to stay in Germany after his discharge. He had nothing much to go home to stateside, so he mastered German and adopted Munich as his new home. Mike was just an occasional drinking buddy, but he actually enjoyed John's company for some intelligent conversation now and then. With a little cajoling and sweet-talk, Mike agreed to let them stay at his tiny Munich apartment.

Mike cautioned the motley pair that he would only put up with them for a couple of weeks, but no more. The offer was downright generous of Mike, but he was seldom at his apartment anyway. He usually stayed over at his girl friend's place across town. John and Pat couldn't believe their incredible luck; they had already found a place to stay! They were both pumped and figured that everything was going to work out just fine. This was going to be a great summer.

****

The following morning, John and Pat went down to the local civilian personnel office. They inquired if there was any summer work that was available in the Munich area. Unfortunately, because it was already early June they were told that it was much too late to apply. All of the available positions had already been filled weeks ago. Bummed by the lack of jobs in Munich, they decided that there were other options they could try. One option was the military resort at Berchtesgaden.

Berchtesgaden is a popular summer tourist destination in the

Bavarian Alps. The U.S. military had their own hotel there where servicemen and their families could stay. John figured that if they couldn't find work at the military resort per se, there were dozens of other hotels, inns and restaurants in the area. Heck, they were willing to do just about anything that paid a regular paycheck. Something was bound to be available there.

Berchtesgaden was some eighty kilometers to the south of Munich. Without any money to spare for train tickets, John and Pat headed for the nearby autobahn exit where they hoped to hitch a ride. As hitch hiking is a safe and common way for young people to get around Europe, it wasn't long before a car stopped and picked them up.

John and Pat spent the next three days in Berchtesgaden, pounding the pavement by day and sleeping on park benches at night. If they didn't find something quick, they wouldn't be eating in another week and a half. In particular, they hoped to find work in a restaurant perhaps bussing tables or washing dishes. That way, they could get free meals during their shifts. Unfortunately, every place they inquired about work turned them away. Perhaps it was just bad luck and bad timing, but more than likely, some clean clothes and a hair cut might have stacked the odds in their favor. Such niceties however, were temporarily out of the question. Despite their best efforts to find honest work in Berchtesgaden, there were no offers of employment.

By the third day, John and Pat were both becoming seriously bummed with their continuing ill fortunes. It had all started so promising just a few days ago; now the winds of fortune had turned decidedly against them. Their finances were drying up and sleeping on benches was getting to be a drag - especially since it had rained the night before. They finally admitted to themselves that the foray to Berchtesgaden had turned out to be a total bust. It was time to head back to Munich. At least in Munich they would have a roof over their heads and a shower – for a while longer anyway. On their way back to Munich, John and Pat contemplated their two remaining options. They could both go home and deal with life there, or they could seek "other" means of employment to see them through the summer.

Chapter 6
Among the Smugglers

Back in those days, several Middle-Eastern car smuggling rings were known to actively operate out of the Munich metro area. It was common scuttlebutt around campus that these operators often recruited drifters, adventurers and cash-strapped college students to help them drive second-hand cars from Germany to Iran. The terms were usually five to six hundred Deutsch Marks and a return ticket to Istanbul. From there, you were on your own to make it back to Germany or wherever. It seemed there were always plenty of young adventurous college kids available during the summer months to take them up on the offer – legal or otherwise.

The operators of these scams ran a very lucrative business; they would buy up used cars in Germany and drive them to Iran and several other middle-eastern countries where they were sold for a very handsome profit. The only problem was that such sales were all made on the black-market. Selling the cars on the black-market circumvented the usually huge 100-200% tariffs normally owed to the governments of those countries to transact a legal import and sale of a car. Understandably, the governments of those countries were not too happy about losing millions in potential revenue from this illicit trade. As the volume of such trade had increased markedly in recent years, the affected countries kept an ever sharper eye on the border crossings.

John and Pat were both well aware that there was a certain level of risk involved in participating in these schemes. In fact several months earlier, some students from the Munich Campus had been caught and jailed in Iran for taking part in this scheme. Shortly afterwards, an article appeared in the Stars and Stripes newspaper describing the operation in detail. It warned other students to beware of such offers; it was illegal and the consequences were serious.

Perhaps dad already had a hunch that this was just the kind of hair-brained scheme that John would naturally gravitate to. After reading the article, dad had wasted no time in picking up the phone and calling John. He specifically warned John "not to even think about it." Naturally, John's answer was a typical teen-aged brush-off to a parental warning, "Yeah dad, don't worry I know better…"

Although dad's stern warning and his promise still rang in his head, John's thinking was becoming heavily clouded by his mounting financial desperation. He had perhaps just enough money to survive another week, maybe two if he kept it down to just one meal a day. Things were very different for him now and the moment of decision was at hand. He had to make a decision quickly. The sensible thing to do would have been to face the reality of the situation and just go home. Perhaps under other circumstances, good sense might have ultimately prevailed, but John had another strong influence close by that heavily skewed his decision making.

During the summer break of the previous year, Pat had succumbed to the lure of adventure and taken his chances on a similar run to Iran. Everything went without a hitch for Pat and he had come back home just fine. Pat had often boasted of what a great adventure it had been and that he would do it again at the drop of a hat. Thanks to his earlier success, Pat was one hundred percent confident they would not have any problems pulling it off again. He had been there and knew the ropes already. Above all, the thought of an adventurous journey to an exotic part of the world was powerful and intoxicating. The truth was that Pat had already quietly decided to himself that he was going again – with or without John. On the way back to Munich, Pat divulged his intentions, "Hey man, I don't know about you but I've decided to do the Iran thing again…are you in?"

John knew the question was going to surface sooner or later. He had wrestled with the issue repeatedly in his mind these past days, but it was now or never. There was no more time left to debate the issue with his conscience. As if looking for a final justification, John muttered, "Well Pat, we're pretty much screwed as it is…" Besides, it just seemed inconceivable to head home to boredom while Pat went on his glorious adventure alone. Pat was his sidekick after all; they had to be in this together. Caught firmly between his growing financial plight and Pat's confident urgings, John finally made the fateful decision to openly disobey dad. "Yeah, what the hell, I'm in."

****

As soon as they were back in Munich, they wasted no time in an urgent bid to hook up with the car runners. John and Pat dumped their bags at Mike's and headed downtown to a stretch of Dachauer Strasse. This was a part of town with a large number of Middle-Eastern immigrants and businesses. At a small café, they struck up friendly conversations with prospective individuals and deliberately let slip that they were "drivers looking for work". Of course when possible, they would mooch free beers and food from generous strangers in the process.

In spite of their best efforts, two crucial days slipped by without making any contacts. To add to the pressure, Mike was getting a little annoyed that the pair was still hanging around his pad with little sign of them leaving anytime soon. When they ran into Mike during one of his brief visits home, he had remarked to them "Haven't you guys found a job yet?" Mike was pretty easy-going, but there was a tinge of irritation in his voice. He wasn't going to put up with squatters in his pad forever. Knowing that their welcome was starting to wear thin, John and Pat reckoned they might get the boot from Mike real soon if something didn't come up fast.

Disappointed at the lack of results and now nearly broke himself, Pat decided it was time to go home to Kaiserslautern for a few days. He had just enough money left for the train fare home. He figured while he was home he could get some clean clothes and a few more dollars from his folks to tide him over until they got their "jobs". Pat's folks were a lot more liberal in that sense; quite unusual for father who was a Colonel in the Air Force.

****

During Pat's absence, John persisted alone in his quest. Two days later, John finally succeeded in making contact with an Iranian named Massoud. Outwardly, Massoud seemed like a legitimate businessman. He claimed to own several businesses in Germany including an import-export company. He told John that he needed a couple more drivers next week for a delivery job to Iran. If John was interested, he would hire him. John's initial excitement immediately turned to dismay when Massoud spelled out the terms. The offer was for a mere 400 Deutsch Marks (about

$250). John was expecting at least 500 or 550 Deutsch Marks. Although he was disappointed at the meager offer, John was now between a rock and a hard place. Saying 'no' just wasn't and option. He figured that beggars can't be choosers and reluctantly agreed to the job. Massoud instructed him to hand over his passport and come back in five days for a final briefing.

That same day, Pat returned from Kaiserslautern. The June afternoon had grown uncharacteristically hot and Pat reckoned it was a good time to grab a cool one. He dropped in at Mathaeser's beer hall to down a liter mug of brew before heading over to Mike's apartment. Pat shared a table and struck up a conversation with a couple unsavory looking guys sitting across from him. Within minutes, Pat learned that these two men were car runners! Elated with the serendipitous contact, Pat wasted no time in calling John to bring him the great news.

John informed Pat that there's a bit of a problem; he's already committed! Sure, his terms were lousy but what could he do? They already had his passport. Disappointed, Pat told John to come down to Mathaeser's any way and meet these guys. Maybe something can be worked out to make the switch. Besides, there was free beer in it for him. That was reason enough.

John headed downtown hopping the bus and U-Bahn (subway). As usual, he didn't buy a ticket as required. John figured that the 60 Deutsch Mark fine for being caught without a valid fare was more than offset by the dozens of free rides he had hitched. In two years time, he had only been snagged once so he figured he was still way ahead of the game. Of course if he got caught now, he wouldn't even be able to pay the fine. No worries though; John was a gambler and the odds were in his favor.

At Mathaeser's, Pat introduced John to Abdullah and Keith.

Abdullah ordered a beer for John. It was his first beer in three days and it tasted especially good on this hot afternoon. John's initial impression of the pair was that they must have been sent from central casting: Abdullah was an obnoxious smelling middle-aged Pakastani with shifty-eyes and sporting a big beer gut. Keith was a skinny, nervous-looking, 20-something American with a murky background which he refused to discuss in any detail. John thought perhaps the guy might be AWOL from the military.

As they sat down to discuss business, the two men made an offer of 600 Deutsch Marks and a ticket back to Instanbul. Now this was a pay scale much more in line with what they were expecting! However, John knew he had put himself in a real quandary with his existing deal with Massoud. These weren't exactly the type of people you want to screw on a deal; they could leave you with some sort of a nasty reminder not to do it again. But Pat urged John to go ahead and take the risk and nix his deal with Massoud. Signing on with Adullah and Keith was a no-brainer, but it would be tricky business getting back his passport in time, if at all. Massoud & Company surely won't be happy to hear that he wanted to back out of his commitment - especially not this late in the game. They were already less than week away from the departure date.

****

John finished his beer and headed out to confront Massoud about his "change of heart". Abdullah and Keith had given John until 6 pm to show up with his passport or else he was out. It was already two o'clock so John had to move fast. On the way there, he decided to give Massoud an excuse about not being able to go because his mother had taken ill. It was lame but as good an excuse as any.

As John expected, there was extreme displeasure from

Massoud at hearing of this news. They had already gone through the hassle and expense of preparing his paperwork and they were not at all happy with John backing out. Losing a driver at this late date meant that they would be forced to leave one car behind. And that would cost them. They did their best to chastise and intimidate John into sticking with his deal. Despite the risk of further irritating these unsavory types, John stood firm on his ground. He wanted out now, and that was that.

Clearly pissed and frustrated at John's stubbornness, Massoud finally relented. He agreed to cut John loose but when John asked for his passport back, he was told that he would get it back in two days. Two days, hell! He needed it back now! John insisted that he wasn't leaving until he got his passport back. Massoud insisted that it wasn't an option so if John wanted to sleep outside his door for two days, he was welcome to.

John decided it was time to play hardball with Massoud. He hinted that if he didn't get his passport back today, he would have to go to the police to report it stolen. This was a veiled threat to blow their cover to the cops if they didn't cough up his passport. John's insolent behavior further infuriated Massoud, but John was beyond the point of no return. Either he got his passport back, or John was totally screwed.

It had come down to a tense contest of wills. Though he put himself at risk, John had pretty much nothing to lose while Massoud couldn't jeopardize his lucrative business. Massoud glared at John, but John had a steely nerve and he wasn't one to be easily intimated. He glared back equally determined. After weighing the pros and cons in his head, Massoud finally flinched and said "Okay, you win" throwing up his hands. In the scheme of things, John just wasn't worth the trouble. He grabbed a piece of paper and scribbled down an address and flung it at John. "You go there" he said angrily. "Now, get out!"

John had won his battle of nerves, but until he had his passport in hand, it would be an empty victory. He was getting desperate as precious time was melting away. The address led John to a printing shop a few blocks away. At the shop, John told the man behind the counter that he was there to pick up his passport. This unexpected request made the proprietor rather nervous as he looked John over. Apparently, John was the first to have come to the shop asking for his passport. Caught off guard, the proprietor asked John to come back tomorrow but John was well beyond messing around. John demanded in an authoritative voice that Massoud told him that he would get his passport today. Maybe it was the tone of John's voice or the mention of Massoud's name, either way John got the man's attention. The man behind the counter was taken aback by John's rather strong demeanor and he motioned John to please wait a moment. He picked up the phone and presumably called Massoud's office for confirmation. He spoke in Farsi and after a brief conversation he hung up the phone looking relieved. He wrote down yet another address for John to go to along with a little map and a brief note. "Everything is okay you go here for passport, yes?" John was beginning to suspect that he was getting the runaround treatment but decided not to say anything. If the guy was lying to him, he knew right where to find him. Besides, it was crunch time and it was imperative that John recover his passport ASAP or risk losing out on both deals. If that came to pass, he would really be screwed! Every minute counted now.

John grabbed the map and headed up town at a brisk pace. The new address led him to a 4th floor apartment a half dozen blocks to the north. A Muslim woman carrying a small child answered the door, John handed the woman the slip of paper and asked for his passport. The woman took a nervous gander past John and scanned the hall in both directions. With that, she motioned John to step inside. She asked John for his name and then disappeared into the apartment.

The dim apartment was cluttered and piled high with boxes and papers and a faint smell of spices permeated the air. Judging by the suspicious demeanor of the woman, these were people who didn't want to be seen or found. They were probably spooked by that fact that some white guy now knew where they lived. Perhaps they were in the country illegally, but John couldn't care less, he just wanted to get his passport and get the hell out.

The woman returned and handed him a brown envelope. John opened it up and there it was; his passport at last. John thanked the woman and made a hasty exit. It was a little after five now and time was fading fast. He hopped the U-bahn again and headed downtown. With precious little time left, he found Pat, Keith and Abdullah still sitting at their booth at Mathaeser's. John had made it in time to make the final cut. He was in!

Chapter 7
Departure for Points East

The morning of June 28th dawned cool and wet. The temperature hung in the upper 50's with a steady drizzle; not an atypical day for Germany in the summertime. John and Pat grabbed their meager belongings and headed for the rendezvous area at the Theresien Wiese just west of downtown. Without so much as leaving their generous host a thank you note, they were on their way. They weren't known for their genteel manners, so they weren't about to start anything that could stain their ill repute.

Theresien Wiese was the giant fairground in Munich where the famed Oktoberfest is held each year. On this gray morning, the grounds were nearly deserted except for a traveling circus tent near the north end. Across the fairgrounds, a small group of cars were clustered together in a parking area. Through the misty rain, John and Pat could see about ten people who had already gathered for the trip.

There was an air of excitement as Keith and Abdullah welcomed the pair as they reported in for smuggling duty. They introduced John and Pat to the seven other drivers hired for the convoy. The others in the group hailed from several different nations and many walks of life: there were two professional drivers, several college students, a couple of drifters and one AWOL Swedish soldier. It was motley crew all right.

Keith and Abdullah had assembled eleven cars of various makes and models for the convoy. John was assigned the blue 1971 Mercedes 200. Keith treated himself to a 1978 Mercedes 280SE, and Abdullah a 1978 Mercedes 200. The others were assigned various 1971-1975 models of Mercedes Benz's including two old 1964 diesels still going strong. In addition, there was a fairly new 1976 BMW 320i, and a 1975 BMW 2002. Everyone could see that the worst car in the bunch was the 1974 VW Super Beetle. Everyone was quietly praying to themselves "please, any car but the Beetle!" To John and Pat's great relief, the consolation prize went to Doug, an Englishman and a truck driver by trade. The endearing bug was not a choice car for an epic overland journey, but like a true Englishman, Doug kept a stiff upper lip with a resolute "All right, then." and took the assignment without complaint.

Before the departure, the drivers were briefed on the convoy rules. They were simple: Always stay in order, keep up with the guy in front and do exactly as they were told at each border crossing. With that, the drivers were released to their respective cars. Without a hitch all eleven cars started up with a roar, and a puff of black smoke from the diesels. With big grins and a "thumbs up" from everybody, Keith led the convoy out of the fairgrounds and on their long journey to Tehran, Iran.

All told, they would be traveling a distance of over five thousand kilometers (3100 miles). This would be no leisurely pleasure tour; instead it would be a marathon journey testing the endurance of the drivers and their cars. On most days, they will have to drive between fourteen to fifteen hours a day for more than a week. Their odyssey would span six countries and two continents. At times they would have to travel some pretty rough roads through rugged and isolated country. John was young, eager and had the stamina to boot. He was more than ready to hit the road to adventure.

Day one:

The rogue convoy left Munich around nine that morning. The rainy weather was a constant nuisance, but the first hour and a half was pure driving pleasure on the German Autobahns. The Autobahns are arguably some of the best high-speed roads in the world and the spectacular scenery of southern Bavaria was a beautiful thing to behold. Everyone was happily cruising along just fine, sometimes hitting speeds of up to one hundred miles an hour. The exception was poor Doug who was struggling mightily to keep up in the Super Beetle.

Everything was going smoothly until they neared the Austrian border crossing near Salzburg. John was jamming to his Pink Floyd's "Dark Side of the Moon" tape when a sea of red brake lights filled the road ahead. Almost immediately, the traffic that was moving so briskly on the autobahn came to a dead stop. For the better part of the next hour, it became a painful bumper to bumper crawl to get to the crossing.

A significant portion of the traffic jam was attributable to the thousands of summer-vacationers from the low-countries. Each summer, tens of thousands of them crowded the popular border crossings headed for the warmer climate of the Mediterranean. It seemed that every single Dutchman in Holland had decided to go on vacation at the same time. The Dutch are a generally likeable people, but this was the one time of year that everyone in Europe cursed them. Not only did they jam up the border crossings, but they often traveled in slow moving caravans on the Autobahns that drove the impatient Germans crazy. It was particularly easy to spot the Dutch; in addition to the required "NL" stickers on their bumpers, it seemed they all drove similar looking sedans pulling identical white teardrop shaped trailers behind them. It was a very "Dutch" thing to do.

Amidst the sea of vacationing Dutchmen and hundreds of other cars and trucks jockeying for position, the convoy soon became scattered in the throngs. Under normal conditions, crossing the border here was a little more than a five minute delay. On this day, it seemed to take forever to reach the checkpoint.

When they finally crossed into Austria, the adjacent rest stops on the autobahn were also jam packed with cars. It was a total zoo with virtually no parking available and cars backed up onto the Autobahn. Keith decided it would be best to pull off onto the shoulder where he could corral the cars as they came through the traffic chaos. Standing in the steady drizzle, Keith flagged each car as it came through the morass. Eventually, the last of the eleven cars made it past the checkpoint and the convoy regrouped successfully.

Just when the convoy was ready to resume the journey, things became further complicated when Keith's car got stuck in the mud. Try as he might, Keith could not get his car out of the mud and back on the pavement. Now in the pouring rain, the members of the convoy pitched in to free Keith's car from the mud. After a good half hour of concerted group effort, Keith's car was finally freed from the grips of oozing mud. This was an ominous start to their journey. The convoy had barely completed the first one hundred fifty kilometers and everyone was already wet, cold and filthy!

To make up for some of the lost time, Keith proposed to the group that they should go further into Austria that evening than originally planned. Late that evening, the convoy pulled into a roadside rest stop in the Austrian Alps. By this time, the cold and wet had taken a physical toll on the drivers. They were all exhausted and ready for some serious shut-eye. Due of the high cost of hotel rooms in Western Europe they would have to sleep in their cars for the night. In fact, they wouldn't even get their first chance to sleep on a cot until they were well into the Balkan countries.

Day Two:

After a fitful night of sleep, the next morning dawned damp and cold. The rainy cold front and the high altitude combined to fill the early morning air with the kind of bone chilling dampness that makes the muscles ache. One by one, the shivering drivers emerged from their cramped cars. This was technically the peak of summer, so almost no one brought jackets or warm clothes with them. John donned his two extra T-shirts and braved the chilly morning air. He then headed straight to the nearby coffee shop for some breakfast and hot coffee.

Thankfully, the rain had let up during the night but the red sky this morning was a sign that more rain was on its way. As the drivers cradled their hot coffee in their hands, Keith called out departure in fifteen minutes. This gave the crew just enough time to scarf down their food and pay a quick visit to the facilities. John wisely kept an empty plastic bottle handy as he figured that the combination of the damp chill and two cups of coffee would be taking a toll on his bladder soon.

The convoy got back on the road and headed towards Graz, in southeastern Austria. Once again, the rainy weather returned to torment them. The rain became heavier and heavier, making the driving conditions extremely hazardous as they snaked their way through the mountain roads. Even under such adverse conditions, the tight schedule meant that the convoy could not appreciably slow down. Any delays this early in the journey could compound itself later costing more time and money. Besides, going through Europe was supposed to be the "easy" part of the journey.

In addition to the stubborn rain, the long winding climbs up to the Alpine passes were especially aggravating to everyone. Often, they were stuck behind slow moving trucks, trailers and tour busses that brought progress to a crawl. At the same time, opportunities to pass were limited and particularly hazardous in this heavy weather.

It was while navigating one of the myriad winding mountain roads, that a large slow-moving semi-truck stubbornly blocked John's progress. The other cars in the convoy had successfully passed it and gone ahead, but the opportunity to pass seemed consistently denied by blind curves and constant traffic. Passing under these conditions was risky business, but at some point John needed to press forward to keep up with the convoy. The on-coming traffic never seemed to let up, or if it did there was yet another blind curve that held him back. John was becoming impatient as he waited and waited for the right moment to pass.

After many frustrating minutes, a window of opportunity finally presented itself. Now was his chance to pass that damn truck! John wasted no time and floored the accelerator as he pulled out to pass. The car's engine whined and strained to build up speed as he began to pull forward alongside the truck. Just then, the lights of another on-coming truck emerged ahead around the curve. Frustrated yet again, John realized that he was not going to make it and decided to drop back. As he tried to pull back in behind the lumbering truck, an aggressive and inconsiderate German had pulled up tight behind the truck. John dropped alongside the other car and muttered under his breath, "C'mon bonehead, let me in…"

John honked his horn and signaled to the other driver, but the idiot driver steadfastly refused to let John slip back in. Falling in further back was out of the question. Lined up behind bonehead was a long line of perhaps twenty cars. John needed to pull back in now and quick! He honked his horn again in a frantic bid to signal the other driver to yield, but the German in all his Teutonic stubbornness still refused to budge!

John was just seconds away from a head-on collision and the oncoming truck flashed its lights in urgent warning. John was completely pissed off now and in a fit of self preservation, he decided he had no choice but to force the issue the hard way. He screamed "You stupid mother fucking Kraut, take this!" and abruptly turned the wheel towards the other car. As John's car came at him fast, Bonehead's eyes grew wide and in sheer panic swerved hard to the right - only to send him self careening off the mountain road! Without a moment left to spare, John reclaimed his rightful place safely behind the truck.

John could hardly contain himself as he raised his middle finger at the other car screamed, "Shit, damn Kraut bastard, damn you!" Down off to his right, he could see Bonehead's car go bouncing down into the valley below and plunging into a shallow riverbed. Aside from just some frayed nerves, no one was killed or seriously injured in this encounter – as far as John knew anyway. John decided that he had served the Kraut Bonehead right and that there was no reason to stop for him. Besides, he had to keep on moving to catch up with the rest of the group.

****

By noon, the convoy cruised past the city of Graz towards the Yugoslavian border. Unlike the chaotic night before, crossing the Yugoslav border was uneventful and everything went smoothly as planned. Within an hour, all eleven cars had cleared the checkpoint and were on their way to Zagreb in Croatia.

About an hour down the road, the convoy pulled over for a break at a small Croatian town. After a bathroom break, the drivers all sauntered over to the local TV shop and joined the crowd of locals standing in the street watching the world cup soccer game in progress. They dwelled just long enough to catch up with the latest score and then it was time to get back on the road. Although driver fatigue was always a constant danger, the tight schedule meant that rest stops like these were far and few in between. The drivers learned quickly to cope with fatigue by eating light snacks and drinking lots of water. Heavy starchy foods were not a good idea at all; they could even be fatal under these circumstances.

Since crossing the Alps, the weather had improved markedly and for this the drivers were most grateful. As they reached the Danube valley, the balmy Balkan summer air felt wonderful in their faces. This was a most welcome change from the cool, damp Northern European climate.

On this second day on the road, the convoy finally reached its destination for the day around two in the morning. It was another no-name road side rest stop, but there were toilets and washrooms and that was good enough. Once again, their accommodations were their cramped cars but the drivers were grateful just to get some sleep. As John curled up in the rear seat of the Mercedes, he wondered how in the hell Doug managed to sleep at all in that tiny Volkswagen Beetle of his. Too exhausted to contemplate anything more, John drifted off into sleep.

Day Three:

After what seemed to be no more than just a few minutes of sleep, there was a loud knocking on his window. Rousted from his deep sleep, John wondered who in the hell was banging on his window in the middle of the night. As he came to, he saw it was already light outside. In fact this was his morning wake up call.

After another light breakfast of pastries and a cup of coffee, Keith had the convoy back on the road by 7:30 am. They drove steadily through central Yugoslavia until mid-morning when the convoy pulled into a gas station to refuel. As each car was refueled, they took off down the road in rapid succession. Keith was already out of sight when the one of the Diesel Mercedes refused to start back up.

John and Pat quickly finished fueling and volunteered to tear after Keith to inform him that there was a car out of commission. They both jumped in their cars and raced down the road trying to catch sight of the lead vehicle. Ironically, in their extreme haste to catch up, neither of them had noticed that Keith's car had pulled off in a field by the side of the road not five hundred meters from the gas station!

As John and Pat went screaming past him, Keith realized that neither of them saw him. Flustered, Keith told Doug to assemble the rest of the convoy there and wait for him. He immediately jumped into his car and took off after John and Pat. Now a mad-cap comic chase was under way with the pursuers being relentlessly pursued!

Keith raced his car furiously until he thought he could see John and Pat's car up ahead in the distance. Meanwhile, having failed to catch sight of Keith's car, John and Pat pushed their cars even faster hoping to catch a glimpse of the lead car. To his amazement, Keith saw the two cars now pull even further away and then disappear altogether! He swore angrily as he stepped on the gas in his desperate bid to catch up but as fast he drove, there was still no sign of them. Keith realized that he was now going dangerously fast. How could he have lost them? He had kept a keen eye out for cars pulled over on the side of the road as well as those going in the other direction. He wondered just how fast those idiots were going!

John and Pat had in fact hit speeds as high as 180 kilometers per hour (120mph) on the two lane highway in hot pursuit of Keith's phantom car! The wild chase finally came to an end almost 100 kilometers later when they entered the town of Nic (neesh). A stoplight in town finally put a halt to the manic chase as Keith finally caught up with John and Pat. Keith pulled alongside John's car and let loose a furious string of choice epitaphs. His face was beet red as the locals now looked on in amusement at the crazy foreigner ranting and raving. Realizing their mistake, John looked back at Pat and let out a feeble laugh. "You were behind us the whole time? Well no shit we couldn't find you!" Keith was the least bit amused by all this, he screamed at them "Now turn your sorry asses around and don't fucking get lost!"

Although the mad chase had ended, the convoy was now scattered for a hundred kilometers and precious time was lost regrouping. Meanwhile, the troublesome diesel had finally come back to life and rejoined the convoy without further problems. Eventually, the tempers cooled down and the group was once again intact.

Late that afternoon, they crossed into Bulgaria and headed for the capital city of Sophia. That evening, the drivers were in for a real treat. For the first time since their departure, they would actually eat a proper dinner and sleep on a cot. At a campground outside Sophia, a couple of bungalows provided a welcome relief after three grueling days of relentless driving and sleeping in cars. That evening, the drivers took advantage of the opportunity to fully rest and relax. As they downed their beers by the campfire, the re-telling of the day's wild chase seemed a lot funnier now. Even Keith was laughing.

Day Four:

Early the next morning, the convoy departed for the Turkish border. At the border crossing, clearing Bulgarian customs was a snap, but entering Turkey with a vehicle proved to be a gauntlet of bureaucratic paperwork and inspections. When it seemed at last that all of his papers were in order, John got back into his car and prepared to proceed on into Turkey. He pulled up to the checkpoint and handed his papers to the guard confident that everything should be in order. The guard looked everything over and returned them satisfied that he was good to go. As John was about to pull forward, another Turkish border guard stepped in front of John's vehicle and with a blast of his whistle, motioned him to stop. The guard then walked over to John and scrutinized him and his car. Wondering what was the matter John nodded in acknowledgement and flashed a friendly smile. The guard took a look around for a moment and then held out his hand towards John and demanded "baksheesh, baksheesh!"

If John wanted to go on his way, he would first have to hand the guard a suitable bribe. Now this was ironic; there he was driving a nice fancy Mercedes but nearly broke at the same time! Just how was he going to get out of this dilemma? Not one to be easily intimidated, John just yelled back "No baksheesh! No money!" The guard was not amused; anyone driving a Mercedes surely must have some extra money to spare. "Baksheesh!" the guard demanded again pointing to his palm. John couldn't give up either for the obvious reason that he was flat broke. The argument bounced back and forth with neither side relenting. The on-going commotion brought the other guards out of their shacks to watch. Clearly, this was the wrong place and time to pick an argument with a Turkish border cop! Actually, there is NEVER a good time to argue with a Turkish cop, let alone refusing a bribe.

John was sinking fast. "Oh crap, I am so busted!" he thought. There he was surrounded by cops, but what the hell could he do? Were they going to just lock him up until he paid up? Damn it all, he really didn't have any money! Just when things were looking pretty grim for John, the guard suddenly changed his tune. Without warning, the cop said "Okay, you go okay" and waved John through. Surprised at the sudden turn of events, John gingerly eased the car forward hoping to tip-toe away from the scene before some other ridiculous crap befell him.

As he slowly cruised away from the checkpoint, a quick look in the rear view mirror revealed the reason for the change-up. While John was distracted by the argument, another much newer and shinier Mercedes had pulled up behind him! Continuing his quest to extort money from the next gullible tourist, the bribe-happy guard quickly stepped in front of the other car. John could see him replaying his spiel again; "baksheesh! baksheesh!" Welcome to Turkey.

After three long hours at the border, the entire convoy finally cleared Turkish customs. They regrouped a few kilometers down the road as was now the routine, and headed for Istanbul. They stopped short of the city to spend another night at a roadside rest stop. Once again their cars served as their hotel rooms; by now John was actually getting used to sleeping in his car.

Day Five:

Early the following day, they entered the city of Istanbul. This ancient city on the Bosphorous was the mid-point in their journey to Tehran. The drivers were granted much of the day to relax and explore the old city. Without hesitation, John and Pat headed for the nearest Turkish bath – it was a welcome, if not a badly needed stop after four long days on the road.

Refreshed and reinvigorated by the baths, they followed up with a visit to the grand bazaar, Tokapi Palace and other historic sites around the town. Good food was also cheap and plentiful here. After a tasty meal of lamb kabobs and local beer, the drivers gathered back at their cars to tackle the second and more difficult part of their journey. That evening, the convoy set out across the Bosphorous Bridge where at mid-span they officially crossed over from Europe into Asia Minor. They drove on again late into the night and then pulled over at yet another anonymous rest stop somewhere in Turkey. By now, the drill was routine; John kicked off his shoes, reclined the seat all the way back, and drifted off to sleep for yet another night in the car.

Day Six:

The next day, they passed through the Turkish capital of Ankara and headed into Eastern Turkey. Eastern Turkey is a beautiful but also a wild and desolate place. As they headed further east, the roads became progressively worse and the weather much hotter. John noticed that with increasing frequency, there were burned out hulks of trucks lying off to the side of the road. The combination of bad roads, bad drivers and poorly maintained vehicles meant that serious accidents were quite common here.

Out here, traffic rules were pretty much non-existent. There was no such thing as waiting your turn or being polite. You either had to be an aggressive road warrior, or you were run off the road. In one instance John was nearly crushed between two trucks. Admittedly, it was a risky move: One truck decided to pass another, but it seemed after it pulled out the truck being passed sped up in some sort of "You can't pass me" game. This went on several times and really tested John's patience. On the third iteration, John saw that there was perhaps just enough room for him to shoot between the trucks! He decided to go for it and the Mercedes' powerful engine shot him into the open slot. Apparently, this maneuver pissed off both truck drivers as they tried to close the gap and crush his car! It was too late though, John's Mercedes slipped through the narrowing gap just in time to avoid damage. The angry truck drivers blew their horns and in return, John gave them the middle finger as he sped ahead and out of sight. After that close call, he switched tactics and started passing trucks and busses on the right hand shoulder. It kicked up a lot of debris and dust each time, but

68

he actually felt safer doing it that way.

On one stretch of a dusty and pot-holed highway, a dust storm reduced the visibility to perhaps 25 meters. John had to swerve repeatedly in the waning light to avoid the large rocks lying in the road. Colliding with one could cause significant damage to his car. It didn't help matters that the Turkish truck drivers refused to dim their Hi-beams for oncoming vehicles either. Perhaps that was another reason for the high accident rate here. For kilometer after kilometer, John expertly dodged the rocks and the blinding trucks until at last his luck ran out. With a loud CRUMP, a large rock cleanly ripped away his entire exhaust system leaving the car blaring uncontrollably like a Harley Davidson. John immediately pulled off to the shoulder to assess the level of damage his car had sustained. He didn't see anything leaking underneath the car and that was good sign. He calmly walked back a hundred meters or so and picked up the various pieces of his car and placed them in the trunk. Without an exhaust system, the car would draw way too much attention to itself at the Iranian border. In fact they may even bar the vehicle from entering Iran altogether. They would have to find a repair shop somewhere up ahead. John fired up the old Mercedes and the car rambled down the dark desolate highway towards the next town.

At the next town, they were directed to the local auto repair shop. It was already getting late, but the shop owner took a quick look at John's car and indicated that it would be no problem to repair it. In Turkey, many auto parts do not come from packages sitting on the shelf. Instead, the resourceful Turks have learned to fabricate almost everything from scratch. The Turks are truly amazing craftsmen. John watched in fascination as they took ordinary piping and sheet metal and created a brand new exhaust system for the Mercedes. In a little less than two hours and all of twenty dollars later, John was back on the road as good as new!

Late that evening the convoy pulled into a closed gas station to line up for gas. Due to the limited availability of fuel in these remote parts of Turkey, it was necessary to park in line at a gas station the night before to insure availability of fuel in the morning. Late arrivals risked not getting any fuel as the stations often ran out – sometimes for days at a time. The next morning the convoy was the first in line for gas so they were able to fuel up quickly and move on out without a hitch. Their goal on this day was to reach the remote hill country of eastern Turkey by nightfall.

Day Seven:

Simply driving through eastern Turkey proved to be quite an adventure in itself. At each rest stop, the convoy drivers were mobbed by enterprising Turks and Kurds who wanted to buy just about anything off the drivers. Aggressive offers were made to buy their cars, their clothes, cigarettes, watches – anything at all. Failing that, they tried to sell you just about anything: cars, clothes, cigarettes, watches, etc. Turks and the Kurds definitely had the entrepreneurial gene.

After more monotonous hours of hard driving on rough roads, the convoy rolled into a small town for a short break. It was already getting dark as the thirsty crew gulped down sodas at a roadside stand. The vendor asked them if they were staying in town that night. When the drivers told him they were driving on to Dagar Baizaia, the vendor shook his head with worrisome dismay. He insisted that it was not safe to drive at night; there were armed bandits roaming the hills nearby. With all of their nice cars, they would be a tempting target. Everyone looked to Keith but he was adamant; they had to make it as far as Dagar Bazaia that night. They had to stay on schedule for the crucial border crossing the next day. In spite of the soft drink vendor's ominous warning, the convoy pressed forward into the waning light. Luckily, they pulled into Dagar Bazaia about 8:30 that night without incident.

Dagar Bazaia was a dramatic setting straight out of the movies. Located at the very foot of Mount Ararat, this region has for centuries been the "Wild, wild east" of Turkey. That night, the drivers were treated to accommodations at a local "hotel". There was no air conditioning, no indoor plumbing, and electricity was unreliable at best, but then again it was the only hotel in town. No one complained though; the drivers were grateful to simply have a real bed to sleep in for the night. The thought of actually being able to stretch out and sleep again was more than enough for John. He would never take pillows and clean sheets for granted again.

After they checked into their rooms, they wandered into town for an evening stroll. A nearby tea shop offered some good food and drink. The prices were so ridiculously cheap here that John helped himself to an extra order of spicy grilled meat. The good, cheap food came at a price though; the ambience wasn't exactly the kind of place to attract tourists. It was hot and dusty and there was an omnipresence of pesky flies that wanted to share his dinner.

As the group ate their dinner and washed it down with sodas, they surveyed their exotic surroundings. They noticed that the town seemed to be a haven for a lot of unsavory types. In fact many, if not most of the residents here were actively engaged in smuggling contraband between Turkey and Iran. John struck up a conversation with a German national who was sitting nearby. He introduced himself as Hans, originally from Deusseldorf. He had been living in Dagar Baizaia for over 10 years already and had no plans to return home. He freely admitted to making a very good, if not unorthodox, living plying the illegal trade. He maintained that life in dusty Dagar Baizaia suited him just fine and that he would probably spend the rest of his life there.

Aside from the smugglers, the rest of the population around town seemed to be mostly well-armed Kurdish tribesmen. The Kurds have long been at odds with the Turkish government. They had an ever simmering resentment for Turkish rule and a burning passion for an independent Kurdistan. From time to time, the Kurds have broken into open rebellion against the neighboring states. Over the years their people have revolted against Turkey, Iraq and Iran. Even during the peaceful times, the desire for rebellion and independence always simmered just below the surface of many Kurds. To this day, this is still the unpredictable and volatile landscape of eastern Turkey.

Day Eight:

Like most summer days in eastern Turkey, the next morning dawned bright, clear and hot. In the early morning light, Mount Ararat appeared stunning as it dominated the scenery of the region. Before departure, some of the drivers decided that another visit to the local Turkish bath was in order. The heat and dust of eastern Turkey quickly took its toll on personal hygiene and they were eager to be rid of their sweaty grime.

After the baths, John, Pat and some of the others decided to take a final stroll around town to take in a bit more of the local color. As he wandered the streets, John was delighted with himself as he was living the adventure he had sought. He bought a couple more sodas and some fruit from the street vendors. This was just the kind of thing that fueled his wanderlust. The kaleidoscope of colorful shops and street merchants filled his senses with the exotic sights, sounds and smells of the Middle East. This was a far sight better than some boring summer job in Munich!

John's wandering thoughts of adventure were rudely interrupted when a loud blast shattered the morning calm. A hand grenade had exploded in a nearby shop not more than fifty meters away. In the ensuing smoke and panic, random gunshots rang out to add to the din. Then as if on cue by some unseen movie director, a general melee' spontaneously erupted in the streets of Dagar Baizaia. Dozens of tribesmen poured into the street and began to tear at each other with knives, sticks and even chairs. John watched with dumbfounded fascination as this scene reminiscent of some Wild West bar brawl unfolded before him. It was just too unreal.

The reasons for the brawl were never clear but John supposed it was some sort of lingering tribal or family vendetta being played out. A few minutes later, truckloads of Turkish troops swept into town and began firing their guns into the air to scatter the rioting masses. John and the other drivers decided that it was high time to make haste for their cars. Getting accidentally shot or arrested could really mess things up. As they ran for their cars, more explosions and gunfire erupted behind them. Pat kept repeating "Oh shit! Oh shit," while John was laughing hysterically at what they had just been witness to. This was getting all too nutty!

Keith was already in his car with the motor running and yelling at everyone to get rolling. As the convoy sped away from town, a bright flash filled John's rear view mirror. A moment later, the car was jostled by the blast. Sure enough, it was the local gas station going up in a ball of flame. There was big trouble brewing in Dagar Bazaia all right. And they had left not a moment too soon.

A few miles out of town, the convoy regrouped to see if there were any casualties or damage. Luckily, all of the drivers had escaped the fracas without a scratch. Just as well, since this was now a critical point in their journey. Beyond the next range of hills to the east was the Turkish-Iranian border crossing. Keith and Abdullah wanted everything to go smoothly as they now prepared to cross the border. If anything were amiss, the border guard's suspicions could be aroused and the entire convoy might be snagged. Each of the drivers in the convoy were now about to become willing pawns in a scheme to violate a statute of the Iranian customs law. John perversely found this fact to be rather exciting. He ribbed Pat, "Hey man, we're gonna be real outlaws now!"

****

A statute in the Iranian customs law required that any vehicle brought into the country of Iran had to be taken back out of the country when exiting. If the vehicle was either sold or left in the country, it then became subject to an import tariff calculated at 200% of the assessed value of the vehicle. For example, a used Mercedes worth ten thousand dollars in Germany might be assessed a value of perhaps twenty five thousand dollars upon import to Iran. Add to this a tariff of another fifty thousand dollars and the legally imported vehicle would sell for at least seventy five thousand dollars or more in Iran. Thus, running illegal cars to Iran and illegally selling them on the black market was a highly lucrative business.

Each year, hundreds perhaps thousands of illegally imported cars were snapped up at bargain prices in Germany and earned a very hefty profit for the smugglers in Iran. The hired drivers were the willing pawns in this game. Most, save for a few of the most gullible hires, knew full well that they were taking part in an illegal activity. Unfortunately for the drivers, it was their own passports that would carry the burden of proof for entering and exiting Iran with the vehicle. If they were caught, their passports would be used as the primary evidence against them. Regardless of the risks, they all placed their trust in Keith and Abdullah as they had successfully made this run at least a dozen times.

Keith gathered the group together to go over the border crossing plan in detail. It was very important that each car arrive and cross the border individually. Their arrivals also had to be at randomly staggered intervals, no less than 20 minutes apart. This was to insure that the Border Guards did not become suspicious that this might be another convoy run by car smugglers. A sharp eyed guard could see the pattern very quickly: Single occupancy vehicles, originating from Germany, and drivers with a variety of foreign passports. The key to success was to appear totally random and hopefully to come upon different guards as they rotated in and out for their shifts and breaks. This would be a tedious process and it would take much of the day to complete. In preparation for their final border crossing the drivers were given a rendezvous point some 20 kilometers inside Iran. With Keith leading the way as usual, the cars departed one by one for the Iranian border some two dozen kilometers away.

John was number ten in the group and Abdullah would bring up the rear of the convoy. The long hot afternoon gave John a chance to catch a nice nap in the shade of his car while one by one, the others moved out ahead of him. In due time, it was John's turn to head for the border. He told Abdullah "See you on the other side" and started towards the border. Along the sparsely traveled road, John cruised steadily towards the border at a reasonable clip. Now was not the time for any screw ups.

****

Everything was going smoothly until seemingly out of nowhere a Turkish cop car appeared in his rear-view mirror and proceeded to pull John over. As the Turkish officer made his way toward his car, John's nerves were a bit edgy. "Damn it!" Thought John "Could this guy have been tipped off? Was the convoy run already compromised somehow? Or maybe they were suspected of having something to do with the mayhem in Dagar Baizaia that morning?" Above all, John was alone now in the middle of nowhere and having another run-in with the Turkish police. John couldn't believe his rotten stinking luck. Indeed this could be some serious trouble. He muttered to himself "Okay, be cool dude".

The officer strolled up to John and without being told to, John greeted the officer and volunteered his license and passport. As the cop looked over his documents, the cop began to ask John some questions in Turkish. John tried to explain that he did not speak Turkish. "Sorry. American…no speak Turkish" said John gesturing as best he could. Unfazed the cop just kept jabbering away at him in Turkish. John struggled to understand what the problem was, "uh, what is problem please? Everything is okay, yes? No speak Turkish." Try as he might, nothing was getting through in either direction. John quickly realized that this cop didn't speak English – apparently not a single word. Failing that, he tried German hoping that might work. "Ich bin Americaner, nicht verstehe Turkish, bitte was ist die problem?" but that too did not communicate at all. There was a serious language barrier here and without a translator, the situation quickly came to a total impasse.

Amazingly, the cop just kept talking away at John as if

nothing were amiss. John was now totally at a loss as to what to do. He couldn't obey the cop if he couldn't even understand what he wanted. He was getting worried that this cop could really upset the apple cart. Everyone else except Abdullah had already crossed over into Iran, and he had to get to the border real soon to stay on schedule. If he got detained by the Turks now, things could really get ugly for him. The rest of the convoy sure the hell wasn't going to turn around and come get him. He was as good as fodder and he knew it.

Oddly, the issue of a bribe had not come up during the encounter. Baksheesh was the one Turkish word John already knew well. This was getting weird; either John was in real trouble and in hot water beyond a simple baksheesh, or perhaps the cop was thinking that with sufficient intimidation, John would volunteer baksheesh to him? If John had twenty bucks on him to spare, he would have gladly paid it and gotten the hell out of there. It was way too critical a juncture for things to go wrong.

After what seemed like an eternity, Abdullah's car came cruising around the bend and pulled up behind John. One thing John knew how to do was to always stay cool under pressure. Upon seeing Abdullah's car, he wanted to jump with joy, but outwardly showed no emotion and said nothing to acknowledge his connection to Abdullah. Likewise, Abdullah acted as if he were just a helpful passerby. Abdullah spoke Turkish fairly well and asked the officer if there was a problem and whether he can be of assistance.

The cop was delighted to finally have a translator available and after a short exchange with the officer, Abdullah turned to John. Abdullah said that the officer has apparently caught him going over the speed limit. The charge was pretty ludicrous considering that in these remote parts of Turkey, speed limit signs were largely absent and the Turks heeded little attention to them anyway. John was driving at a good clip, but nothing unreasonable or unsafe for such a remote stretch of road. John estimated that he was probably doing about 80 km/hr. Besides, he hadn't seen a speed limit sign all day. How was he expected to know what the speed limit was here anyway? The officer responded by informing John that the speed limit on this stretch of highway was 45km/hr (about 28 mph!). This was just absurd! This was an isolated stretch of rural highway! John demanded to know where it was posted as such. 45km/hr was just ridiculous!

Not to be distracted by such details, the officer claimed that John was nonetheless caught exceeding the limits, posted or not, and therefore he must pay a fine. The officer demanded $200 US – paid in cash immediately! Abdullah turned to John and nonchalantly told him "He wants you to pay him a fine of two hundred dollars U.S. Just tell him you don't have any money." Being nearly broke as he was, John could only oblige Abdullah's suggestion.

"No money, no lira, no dollar!" said John shaking his head. Saying "No" to Turkish cop wasn't a good idea under any circumstances, but what else was he to do? Undaunted, the cop continued his extortion attempt without making any headway. All John could say was "no" over and over. As they reached yet another impasse, the cop curiously reduced the amount of the fine to $100. That was better, but even that amount was still out of the question. John's answer was still "no". This entire exchange was going nowhere. After more minutes of this fruitless back and forth haggling the attitude of the cop soon began to go from a commanding tone to a noticeably more receptive tone.

Eventually the encounter deteriorated into full fledged negotiation with the cop losing badly to John. As the minutes passed, the amount of fine continued to drift downward. Could John pay $50? How about even $10? Finally, in an act of final desperation, the cop pulled out his wallet to show John and that he too had no money! He then showed John a picture of his family while rubbing his stomach and moaning. This was absolutely amazing! The poor cop was now reduced to begging for a handout so he could have money to feed his family! In the end, a final settlement amount was reached. John forked over a grand total of three dollars and fifty cents and was released to go his way.

****

Delayed by over thirty minutes due to the pesky cop, John finally arrived at the Turkish/Iranian border crossing. He kept his cool and keenly observed that everything appeared normal as he drove up to the crossing. Clearing customs on the Turkish side involved mostly counter signatures on his papers and things went a lot quicker than it was getting in. He also got his passport stamped including one that read, "Exit with automobile" and he was good to go. So far, this was a piece of cake and John was just glad to be out of Turkey after the run-ins he had had with the law there. Thankfully, there weren't any more bribe-demanding border guards to deal with this time.

Over on the Iranian side, the process was somewhat more thorough. Vehicle and engine serial numbers were documented in addition to the usual registration, insurance and tags. Next to his entry stamp into Iran, an endorsement "entry with automobile" was added. It was a long and trying afternoon for John, but in the end all of the vehicles passed safely through without a hitch.

At the rendezvous point, the drivers passed high-fives all around as they had cleared the final hurdle on their way to Tehran. Then it was back on the road again racing across the western Iranian desert towards the city of Tabriz and beyond. As they passed through Tabriz that evening, John and Pat paid scant attention to this obscure city in Northwestern Iran. Little did they imagine that this passing milestone on the road to Tehran would soon become a place they would come to know intimately. For the moment though, their thoughts were focused on reaching Tehran, and Tabriz was quickly forgotten as a place of no special significance. The weary group pushed on past midnight and then finally pulled into another welcome stop at a real hotel. This time, there was running water and there was electricity on demand. Life was good here.

Day Nine:

The following day, the anticipation of reaching their final destination ran high. It had been a grueling week-plus trip and the drivers were ready for a break. Thankfully, as the convoy closed in on Tehran the roads became much better. The final two hundred kilometers even offered the luxury of a modern multi-lane superhighway. Now this was civilization once again! Near the town of Zanjain, the group pulled off the main road to enjoy a refreshing dip in the Zanjain River. The drivers were all smiles as the cool clear waters of the river brought welcome relief from the relentless heat and dust. All too soon though, their jovial R&R was over as they all piled back into their cars to make the final dash to Tehran.

Late that afternoon, the convoy finally entered Tehran proper. Their destination was the Tehran International airport, the final delivery point for the vehicles. When they reached the airport, the cars were driven to a far corner of the parking lot. For the hired drivers their grueling journey was finally over. As they emerged from their cars for the last time, there was a chorus of whooping it up followed by an impromptu celebration of soda pop, high fives and snapshots. It was mission accomplished! John felt elated. What an adventure it had been! Pat was right all along.

Tomorrow morning, the customers who were promised these cars would start arriving to claim their vehicles. Now it was time for the drivers to clear out before they attracted too much attention. Nine of the cars were secured for customer pick up while the rest of the crew piled into the two remaining cars for the drive downtown. They would be staying at a budget hotel for a couple of days until they were ready to leave. Keith explained to everyone that he needed those two days to have their passports "fixed" so they could leave the country without any problems. The drivers were more than happy to take advantage of this downtime to really relax, enjoy some good meals and do a little sightseeing around town.

Chapter 8
Accidental Tourists

In the summer of 1978, there were already rumblings and rumors of big political troubles to come in the land of the Peacock Throne. Anti-Shah and anti-American sentiment was growing rapidly around many parts of the country. Despite the disturbances, John and Pat found Tehran to be generally friendly and welcoming. They figured that they would be back in Germany in a couple of weeks at most, so these regional political problems were of little concern to them. In view of the moment, their lack of concern for their safety was completely understandable. As the passage of time and events would soon prove, they could not have been more wrong.

Two days later Keith returned with everyone's passports as promised. Each of the passports has been expertly "fixed" by a local forger. The "entry with automobile" stamp issued at the Iranian border had vanished and the same area had been stamped over by some bogus visa stamp to prevent arousal of suspicion. It was also payday as the drivers received their well-earned money and their tickets home.

In the elation of the moment, none of the drivers took any notice of the inconsistency on their passports: Although the "entry with auto" stamp had been neatly removed, the "exit with automobile" stamp issued on the Turkish side of the border was left untouched. This inconsistency would not pose a problem for those who chose to fly home, or leave Iran via other neighboring countries such as Afghanistan or Pakistan. The passport checks at the airports almost never scrutinized for auto entry/exit stamps. On the other hand, border guards stationed on the eastern borders along Pakistan and Afghanistan often could not read Turkish. The language issue probably played a large part in Pat's successful run the year before. On that trip, Pat had exited through the Iran-Pakistan border to the east instead of going back through Turkey. For John and Pat this minor oversight would soon prove to be their Achilles' heel. They had already made their fateful decision to head for Istanbul by train.

With their task completed and cash in hand, the drivers all bid their farewells to one another and went on their separate ways. Many of these guys were drifters, chronically addicted to a life of drifting from adventure to adventure. True to their nature, a few of them planned to fly out to various new destinations, while some of the others chose to go to India by bus. A couple of them even planned to stay in Iran for a while and seek out local jobs.

****

In keeping with their original plans to take the train home, John and Pat headed for the main train station to make their reservations. They had hoped to be on their way within the next few days, but instead they were floored when they learned that the first open seat on an outbound train wouldn't be available for four more weeks! Stunned by the unexpected and lengthy delay, John and Pat decided to find a cheap hotel in town and wait out the duration. Flying home was considered, but the high cost of plane tickets to Europe would eat up all of their hard-earned cash and then some. Besides, what fun would that be anyway? They were adventurers!

That afternoon, they were able to find tolerable lodgings at a nearby budget hotel. For about two dollars a day, they would have a place to sleep and wash up. The room had no air conditioning, but there was indoor plumbing and the sheets were changed once a week. That was plenty good for them.

During the coming days, John and Pat walked the streets of Tehran to pass the time. They spent a good deal of time meeting and chatting with the locals at teahouses and public squares around the city. Once again, they took advantage of the middle-eastern hospitality when offered in order to stretch their finances. The food here was good and plentiful and with plenty of good-hearted Iranians around, they were in no danger of going hungry. A couple of young students even volunteered their time to be impromptu tour guides, showing them the historic sites around the city. With so much unsolicited generosity offered to them, they found it hard to reconcile their daily experience with the rabid anti-American hatred that the media reported regularly.

One day, they also decided to look up Senior Airman Owen, an American they had met at last year's Oktoberfest. All they had was his name, rank and that he was stationed in Tehran at the time. They figured it would be worth the effort and went down to the nearby U.S. base to see if they could track him down. Luckily, Senior Airman Owen was still stationed there. Owen was pleasantly surprised to see the duo again and offered to buy them a couple of beers. When Owen heard that they were stranded in Tehran for a spell, he offered them some hospitality, courtesy of the U.S. Air Force. This lucky break gave John and Pat some welcome access to the base NCO club and its recreational facilities. They were most grateful that they could spend much of their remaining time hanging out at the NCO club pool to get relief from the midday heat. If they weren't hanging out by the swimming pool, they were inside shooting pool in the air conditioned lounge. Now this was more like it – it was almost like vacationing at a nice resort! They had scored big; not bad for a couple of cash-strapped kids stranded in a foreign country.

Eventually the long days finally melted away and the departure date rolled around. It had been a great summer adventure - perhaps the adventure of a lifetime, but now they were more than eager to head back home to familiar territory. They checked out of the little hotel that had been their home for the past month and headed to the train station. Along the way John and Pat talked about the great stories they would tell their friends when they got back home. Little could they imagine that the real adventure was only now beginning.

Chapter 9

Homeward Bound

At long last, they boarded the train bound for Istanbul. When the train finally pulled out of the station, John was happy to be going home. He had experienced enough adventure to keep him satiated for a while. Besides, these past weeks had been pretty lean at times and he was ready for some of mom's good home cooking. It was still a long journey home though; their tickets would only take them as far as Istanbul. From there, they would have to wing it – mostly by hitch hiking. It would probably be a good couple of weeks before they would make it all the way home.

As the suburbs of Tehran melted away and the train headed into open country, John got up to check out the rest of the train. This was no Orient Express, but to his satisfaction he found the train fairly modern and clean. Oddly, the menu in the dining car consisted of a single item – a TV dinner of sorts. Not that it mattered, as John and Pat had loaded up on fruits, snacks and drinks to save money.

The train stayed on schedule and moved along at a healthy clip. Outside their window, the scenery was beautiful as the setting sun illuminated the mountains to the north. The only downside was that second class tickets meant sitting on hard wooden bench seats for the next twenty plus hours. Not much fun, but they were very used to Spartan accommodations by now so they would fare just fine. Late that evening, the train would cross the border into Turkey. Not that John or Pat gave it much thought, but the border crossing was technically their final hurdle on their way home. Once they were past it, they were home free. Soon, the gentle rocking of the train and the rhythm of the rails lulled John into sleep.

****

Some eight hours later, the train pulled into the city of Tabriz. It was dark when they had passed Tabriz the first time on their way to Tehran, and it was dark again. Not that it mattered as it was simply a waypoint on their journey. At Tabriz, the train took on a lot more passengers and it became quite crowded, almost full. Along with the passengers, several immigration and customs officers boarded the train. From here, it was a two and a half hour run through the western Iranian desert to the Turkish border.

Shortly before 10pm, the train departed Tabriz and began the run for the Turkish border. A few minutes later, the customs agents began making their way through the train to collect passports from all of the passengers. John and Pat played it cool as they were asked to produce their passports. They calmly handed them over, fully trusting that the "fix" would get them through.

About forty minutes later, two of the customs officers came back into the car. They held two passports in their hands, presumably John and Pat's. The ranking officer paused in the aisle before them and said "Mr. John Burchill and Mr. Patrick Tiahrt?"

"Yes, that's us" said John wondering what was up.

Speaking in the King's English the officer said, "Gentlemen, I must inform you that there is a 'little problem' with your passports."

"Uh, problem? What problem would that be?" muttered John.

"I would like to know what you did with your cars."

This was a moment of total adrenaline rush; John and Pat knew they had been terribly busted. Damn it, this was NOT supposed to happen! In fact they were so sure that they would never get caught that they had no ready alibi on hand, no neatly concocted "plan B" to fall back on. In this moment of sheer panic and desperation, the only words that stumbled out of John's mouth were "um, what cars?"

The sharp-eyed customs officer had caught the irregularity of the auto endorsement stamps. He knew right away that something was amiss with these two young Americans and he wanted an explanation. The heat was on big time, and they had to come up with ANY STORY however incredulous – and RIGHT NOW! Either they were going to be able to talk their way out of this, or they were in serious trouble! John glanced over at Pat and he could see that Pat was already coming apart at the seams. Pat's hands were trembling uncontrollably as he lit up a cigarette. His body language was screaming "I'm guilty!" It was up to John to take charge. Under the intense pressure of the situation, John made his best effort to stay cool and to concoct pure fiction on the fly. John began to explain to the officer that the reason they don't have any cars with them is because…

"Well, that's because we were both involved in a bad accident just inside Turkey." John said, not quite sure of the next thing to say.

"An accident? At the border?"

"Ah, yes it was just about ten kilometers from the Iranian

border."

"And you are saying that both cars were damaged at the same time?" The officer already smelled a dead rat in this fable.

"Uh, yes…both cars." John's mind was going a million miles per hour.

The officer crossed his arms, his body language was screaming let's hear you bullshit your way out of this one, buddy! "I see, so please, tell me exactly what happened?"

John was totally impressed with himself that he was holding his own under such pressure. On the other hand, Pat was looking pale like he was going to throw up all over the place. John explained, "As it so happened, I was driving along on a narrow curve when I saw this oncoming truck that was passing another truck. I slammed on my brakes quickly to avoid a crash with the truck, but my friend Pat here, he didn't see me stop in time and crashed into the back of my car so hard that both cars were damaged very badly – beyond repair."

"I see, and then what did you do with the cars may I ask?" The officer was finding this tale quite incredulous but entertaining.

John continued, "Ah well, since we were very close to the Iranian border and we wanted to leave Turkey – you know, without all of the legal problems of disposing ours cars there, we had to figure out a solution."

"And what was the solution?"

The first thought that had popped into John's head was the rampant bribery he had endured in Turkey. Without having the benefit of time to weigh the wisdom of his words, John just reflexively spat out, "Well, in Turkey do as the Turks do right? So we paid the Turkish customs officer to stamp our passports so that we could leave Turkey without our cars." John was on a roll and made sure to close with emphasis, "And that sir, is why there are no auto entry stamps from Iran customs – because we had no cars at that point!" John had even amazed himself that he whipped out that tall tale as quickly as he did.

Unfortunately, the customs officer was not at all amused with this, "So, you say you bribed a Turkish official?

John suddenly realized his little "bribe" spin was not going over well at all so he quickly clarified that comment, "Of course, I would never do such a thing in Iran. The Iranian officials aren't corrupt like those Turkish officials, no sir!"

It was a nice try on John's part, but no dice. The officer wasn't buying it for one second. "I am very sorry for the inconvenience gentlemen, but I must inform you that I will have border guards waiting to take you into custody at Razi Crossing. Please be prepared to disembark, thank you gentlemen." With that and a slight tip of his cap, the officer walked back to the conductor's quarters. By now all eyes in the car were burning holes into the backs of their heads. Their expectations for a graceful exit from Iran had misfired horribly. In a matter of minutes, their plans for going home were crushed.

Chapter 10
Razi Crossing

It was close to midnight when the train came to a halt at Razi Crossing. The Customs officer and his aide came back to escort them off. "This is where you get off gentlemen. Please follow me." John had not expected Razi Crossing to be such a forlorn place. Why there was no town here at all! It was pitch-black in every direction save for a couple of lights illuminating just one small building. Razi Crossing was nothing more than a whistle stop smack in the middle of nowhere.

As they stepped off of the train, three border guards took custody of them. One of them, the officer in charge exchanged a few words with the customs officer on the train. With that, the customs officer gave his signal and the train slowly began to pull away. John and Pat knew they were in the proverbial "deep doo doo" now. Pat almost lost it as they helplessly stood there and watched as the train disappeared into the darkness. It was a feeling of utter abandonment. As they were led away towards the lone structure, John knew that even if they somehow managed to talk their way out of this mess, the next train was still weeks away. One way or the other, they were seriously screwed!

The border guards escorted the pair into the solitary building where they were held in the waiting room. Meanwhile the officer in charge telexed Tabriz for further instructions on what to do with the unexpected arrivals. Despite the nerve-wracking situation, John put on his best airs to stay calm and did a pretty convincing job at it. Already, John was thinking the situation over and seeking options. Pat on the other hand continued to sweat profusely and chain smoke like mad - all the while his hands shaking uncontrollably. He sat on the wooden bench in a fetal position, rocking back and forth, all the while mumbling to himself, "We're so screwed, we are so screwed." After a while, Pat's lack of intestinal fortitude was really starting to irritate John. John couldn't contain himself any longer and finally yelled at Pat; "Knock it off you asshole, you're making us look guilty as hell."

"Man, I'm sorry…I'm sorry, I'll shut up," muttered Pat, but the scolding did absolutely no good; Pat just kept right on chain smoking and muttering to himself.

While John and Pat pondered their fate in their own characteristic ways, their assigned guards found ways to battle their own boredom. They started goofing around by pointing their presumably loaded guns at each other and engaging in a mock gunfight. Apparently they were under the impression that they were providing entertainment for the detainees. They danced around the room yelling "Chicago gangster! Al Capone! Bam bam bam bam"! John and Pat weren't amused as they had other pressing issues on their minds. John just smiled at them and wished they would knock it off before the damn things went off and killed one of them. Besides, he couldn't even think clearly while they were making such a damn racket.

Three nerve-wracking hours later, the senior officer finally walked back into the room. With a lump in their throats, they both braced themselves in anticipation of the bad news. The officer spoke in reasonably good English "My gentlemens, ah…I am very sorry for you." He held the telex from Tabriz headquarters in his hands. "eh, very big mistake for you. Very big mistake."

John was thinking to himself "yeah, I know we made big mistake, and my ass is sorry too. So quit rubbing it in." When John heard the next words from the officer's mouth, it took a moment to register.

"Now you can go free, gentlemens. Not arrest you today. Mistake, yes mistake" he was pointing to the telex and smiling.

There was a moment of silence as the officer's last words finally registered in their already overstressed minds "Say, what?" John uttered. Everything seemed so incoherent now.

The officer smiled and handed them their passports. "You go free, yes."

John and Pat looked at each other and spoke almost in unison "We're free to go now?"

"Yes, yes, now you may go."

John and Pat looked at each other in disbelief again. This was freaking amazing! Their detention was all a mistake? They were free to go! Wahoo! This was awesome news, but where could they possibly go at this hour? It was sweet to be free again, but the liberty was almost meaningless at the moment. It was 3 am and in the stinking middle of nowhere and there won't be another train for at least a week! And that was assuming that the train would have an available seat. Just what in the hell could they do now?

John and Pat quickly pondered their other options. They had been miraculously released from the yoke and their first impulse was to run frantically for the border. They figured they could walk along the tracks over to the Turkish side and then hitch a ride from there to the nearest town. That sounded like a feasible option so they stepped outside and peered into the forbidding darkness to survey the route.

Freedom was just a few hundred meters to the west, but aside from the single light glimmering in the distance, it was pitch black everywhere. To make matters worse, they were in the middle of bandit country. If the bandits didn't get them, the Turkish guards just might shoot them dead by mistake. Imagine a couple of Yankee white boys walking around in the darkness in the middle of the Iranian desert at 3 am in the morning. Indeed anything could happen out there including being arrested on the Turkish side for lord knows what. Their unorthodox arrival was bound to raise some real suspicions.

The more they thought about it, the more they realized this was not a good place to be wandering about at that hour. Everything ran counter to their instincts to flee, but they were faced with a real dilemma and neither option was very appealing. In the end, staring into the darkness and unknown threats was just too foreboding. They finally decided that it was best to go back inside and wait until first light to cross.

They walked back in to the waiting room at Razi and motioned to the guards that they wanted to sleep there that night. They laid out their sleeping bags on the wooden benches and crawled in. Totally exhausted from the stressful events of the day, they both fell asleep quickly.

****

It must have been around 8 in the morning when John and Pat were rousted from their deep sleep. The officer on duty informed them that Tabriz headquarters had sent a follow-up message. He was terribly apologetic as he explained to them that headquarters wanted to have the suspects brought in to Tabriz for questioning after all!

He spoke with a distressed face while gesturing to the new telex he had received. "eh good morning gentlemens, eh I am very sorry…eh, Tabriz say I make you arrest now."

John's mind was still a bit foggy from his slumber and it took a moment to process what he had just heard. "What? Arrested? You told us were free to go!" John said incredulously. "You've got to be kidding!"

"No make joke…so sorry, sorry."

The sickening realization of their cruel twist of fate brought knots back to their stomachs again. This was just unbelievable! They had made one horrible, horrible mistake! A few hours ago, freedom was theirs for the taking and now they had let it slip through their fingers! There was no one to blame but themselves. Pat was turning pale again and started to look for his cigarettes. He started muttering to himself uncontrollably again. "This isn't happening man, this can't be happening, tell me this isn't happening…oh shit, oh shit…."

John kept it curt, "Of all the rotten, stinking, miserable luck! Damn it!"

****

Around 9 am, John, Pat and the two guards piled into a Toyota Land Cruiser. They headed out across the wide western Iranian desert towards Tabriz. There were no roads in this area so they had to drive for hours along bumpy riverbeds and dusty desert tracks. The going was painfully slow and uncomfortable. Not that it mattered much, but the two young guards promptly fell asleep within the first fifteen minutes.

The driver was a middle-aged man who decided on his own

to take the two American "guests" on an impromptu tour of the area. He spoke decent English and with typical Iranian hospitality, he went out of his way to narrate points of historical interest to the pair. He even offered to stop if they would like to get out and take pictures. John thanked the driver for his generosity, but he explained that they were not too concerned about getting pictures on this trip. Under any other situation, John would have taken more interest in the region's history, but on this day he had other pressing thoughts on his mind.

After bouncing across the wide desert landscape for hour after hour, the Toyota finally pulled into Tabriz headquarters at around eight that evening. Upon arrival, the exhausted pair was taken into an office instead of a holding cell. There, they were instructed to lay their sleeping bags on the office floor for the night. The office manager bade the pair good night and locked them in until morning. Despite the long drive and fatigue from stress, neither of them could sleep that night. Instead, they stayed up into the wee hours of the morning rehearsing their alibis repeatedly. They had to make sure the details of their stories were in perfect sync for the interrogation the next day.

Chapter 11
Home Front

Back home in Germany, our family waited and wondered about John's whereabouts. The last communication from John was a postcard mailed from Munich dated June 22nd. In it, he wrote:

"Dad,

This is a kind of inappropriate post card but it was all I had. As I write this, I'm on my way to Tehran. I'd really much rather get a job, but it was not quite available at this time, and I'm flat broke so I decided to go there. The terms are 600 Marks cash, all expenses paid (motel, food, etc.) and a ticket back to Istanbul. Tell Mom not to worry and I'll call when I get back (about 1 month).

-John

P.S. I'll drop a post card or two on the way down.

There we were, already in the last week of July. According to his post card, John should have been back from Iran by now. There had been no other postcards or letters since the initial communication. If he was back, he would have called home. Perhaps something had happened to delay him, but we had no way to contact him. All we knew was that he was "out there" somewhere between Iran and Germany and that was a lot of territory.

Around that time, my mother told me that she had a terrible dream a couple of nights before. In her dream, she saw John calling for her across a void, but something kept holding him back. Try as he might, he could not cross over to her. Knowing her tendency to worry too much – as all mothers do, I tried to reassure her that her fears were working overtime. But she was sure something bad had happened to John. I tried to play it down and put on my best face, but I knew from experience that my mother could be at times chillingly clairvoyant. I too had a nagging feeling that bad news might be coming soon.

We didn't have to wait much longer. On the afternoon of July 28th, my dad received the dreaded phone call from Mr. Mellon of the American Consulate in Tabriz. Dad was informed that John Burchill and Pat Tiahrt had been arrested and that they were being detained by the Iranian authorities at Tabriz headquarters on charges of "alteration of passport stamps" and "customs violation." When I heard the news, I felt a knot in my stomach and my mother burst into tears and cried all day and night. I wondered that day if I would ever see my crazy but beloved brother again. I knew the coming months and probably many years would be a difficult time for all of us. We expected incarceration for sure, but for how long was an open question. This news alone was hard on all of us, but at that time we had no idea what a real trial by fire ordeal it would later become.

Chapter 12

Outlaw Guests

After a long and sleepless night, the voices out in the corridor returned. The sound of the door to the office being unlocked seemed menacingly loud after a night of quiet conversation. This was a morning neither of them looked forward to but each had braced themselves for throughout the night. Instead of a grim dawn, the office manager greeted them with a hearty "Good morning, Good morning, my American friends!" Though tired from lack of sleep, the unexpectedly friendly greeting took the edge off for John and Pat. They returned a cordial "Good morning to you, sir" hoping to stay on the good side of everyone. They wanted to take every opportunity to make sure they made a good impression. Maybe, just maybe, they would be seen as just a couple of dumb kids who were duped into doing something illegal. After all, they weren't really "bad" like the real hardcore criminals were. As they rolled up their sleeping bags, the duty officer informed them that they would be interrogated by the chief inspector of the customs police that morning.

It was shortly after ten that morning when a guard entered the room and looked over at John and Pat. After a couple of words with the duty officer, the guard approached the pair. Perhaps it was the unrestrained look of sheep going to slaughter on Pat's face that made him the first choice to go in for questioning. The guard pointed to Pat and ordered "You, come please." As Pat got up, John reminded Pat "Hey don't worry man. Just tell it like it happened, got it?" Of course John meant "Just stick to the agreed story".

Truth be told, John was nervous as hell about Pat going first. In tough situations like this Pat always came up short on intestinal fortitude. Unfortunately, this day would prove no different. After about forty five minutes, Pat was led back into the holding room looking like he had finally thrown up – at least metaphorically if not literally. The guard then motioned to John "You next please". As John stood up to go, he asked Pat nonchalantly, "You told them the facts right?"

Pat hung his head shamefully and admitted that he had spilled the beans on everything. "Sorry man, I told them everything."

What! All that planning and rehearsing down the toilet already! John was so livid inside that he could have wrung Pat's neck at that moment. Instead, all he could do was to mutter under his breath, "Pat, you're nothing but a goddamn chicken shit jerk, you know that?"

Left with no choice but to follow suit, John confessed likewise to the inspector. As John's temper cooled, he figured that bogus story about crashing the cars inside Turkey was a bit far-fetched anyway. Any good interrogator would have seen right through that BS line and checked the facts. It was just as well that Pat told the truth to avoid getting them into deeper trouble. That thought calmed John down and the rest of the interrogation passed quickly.

The Chief inspector was an astute man; he had quickly figured out that these were just a couple of young kids looking for adventure. They were the little fish and quite harmless, but nonetheless they had broken Iranian law and they would have to be held accountable for their part in the acts. After John's part of the interrogation was over, Pat was brought into the room and seated next to John. They were told that their actions have broken certain statutes of Iranian Customs and Passport law. Tomorrow, they would be taken to see the district prosecutor to have their charges formally filed.

It was coming up on noon now. Before sending the two suspects back to the detention room, the Chief told John and Pat not to worry; they would be well taken care of while in his custody. Indeed the Chief inspector held good to his word and called over the head guard. He handed the guard some Rials with instructions to take the young "guests" into town for a good meal.

Officially, two guards were assigned to take John and Pat out to lunch. However as the word got out, several more eagerly volunteered to take the Americans out to town. Chaperoned by a half-dozen guards as if they were VIPs, John and Pat were driven into town for lunch. The restaurant was actually quite nice and having survived on marginal finances for weeks, John and Pat eagerly ate their fill. Besides, this was some really good Iranian cuisine!

The guards were also having a great time dining out with their American "guests". They asked seemingly endless questions about what it is like to live in "Amerika" and repeatedly mentioned that they would like to go live there someday. The irony of the situation was not lost on John and Pat as they echoed that they too, would like to be going to America – rather than to an Iranian jail. With that, they all shared a good laugh and even Pat was now smiling for the first time in couple of days. For all they knew, this could be their last decent meal for a long time to come, but at least it was very satisfying and with unexpectedly enjoyable company.

****

After lunch, the two were driven back to police headquarters. Expecting the bizarre honeymoon to end any moment now, the surreal then gave way to the ludicrous. Instead of returning them to detention, the guards now beckoned John and Pat to come out and play volleyball with them! This was a far sight better proposition than sitting in detention so John and Pat eagerly obliged their request. They pitched in to help put up the volleyball net and the game was on.

Amazingly, the guards all took off their gun belts and piled their weapons on a table not more than ten feet from John and Pat. John couldn't help but think; if they were going to make a break for it, this would be the time! Then again, better sense prevailed and John decided that it probably would not be such a good idea as they were in enough trouble already! The temptation was finally removed when one of the more sensible guardsmen looking on decided to move the guns to a safer place.

After a fun-filled afternoon of volleyball, they sought some shade to escape the afternoon heat. John and Pat joined their guards for some cool drinks. They chatted a while more and then one by one, the guards laid down for a little afternoon nap! This was too much but who were they to argue with protocol? John and Pat curled up and joined the guards in dreamland.

As evening rolled around, the love fest wasn't yet over; the happy entourage once again piled into the jeeps and headed back into town for dinner. On the way, John leaned over to Pat and whispered, "Being under arrest like this ain't half bad."

****

Next morning, John and Pat were driven down to the central courthouse in Tabriz to meet with the prosecutor. When they arrived at the courthouse, it was something of a madhouse; there were dozens of Iranians screaming and yelling at each other in the halls. It seemed everyone was engaged in a heated argument with someone else. With passions running high everywhere, John thought that they had happened upon a high profile murder trial or something but apparently, this was all quite a normal day at the courthouse.

The guards seemed to heed little notice of the chaotic crowd as John and Pat were led down the crowded hallway. Outside of the prosecutor's office, a loud and unruly mob crowded the entrance making it almost impossible to get though. Each time the door to the prosecutor's office opened the crowd chaotically surged forth trying to enter as the guards fought to hold them back. Apparently there were a lot of people with grievances who had been waiting for days to speak to the prosecutor. It was quite a spectacle.

Their guards forced a path through the crowd and unlike the locals John and Pat were let in without delay. Inside the office was sanctuary compared to the mayhem just outside the door. The office was spacious and furnished tastefully with fine furniture. The prosecutor greeted the pair with a "Bonjour, messeurs". Caught off guard by the French greeting, John and Pat reciprocated with "Bonjour" although neither spoke any French. The prosecutor was a very distinguished looking gentleman and looked dapper in his fine Italian suit. He motioned for the pair to sit down on the leather couch and then offered each of them a Coke and a pack of Dunhill cigarettes. Clearly, he was a man of fine taste and sophistication.

The prosecutor's aide welcomed the pair and asked them if they might be able to conduct the meeting in French? He explained that the prosecutor spoke fluent French but very little English. French was definitely out for John and Pat so they asked the assistant to interpret for them. He said that would be just fine.

The prosecutor began by asking what brought them there. Aside from the occasional question to clarify details, he listened politely as John and Pat told their story. While admitting to their actions, John and Pat made sure to spin their story so that they would be perceived as unwitting victims more so than willing accomplices. They were careful to qualify their answers with phrases like "we were duped…" and "we were lied to, mislead…" etc. John hedged that the prosecutor would be more interested in getting at the ringleaders rather than their pawns. By keeping the spotlight focused on Abdullah and Keith and playing the victim card wisely, John hoped to gain some leniency from the prosecutor. With a little luck and sympathy from the prosecutor, the charges they faced might be reduced or better yet, dropped altogether. As the meeting unfolded, the prosecutor took everything in stride and the atmosphere remained very cordial and at times, light-hearted. Encouraged by the positive tone and flow of the meeting, John and Pat wrapped up their story with high hopes that they just might get off easy.

The prosecutor lit another Dunhill, and leaned back in his chair but didn't say anything. Perhaps he was contemplating letting them go in exchange for the information they provided about the car smuggling operators. The cordial treatment that they had received from the police during the past day had unfortunately greatly inflated their expectations of getting off easy. They had lulled themselves into a false sense that the crimes they were being charged with were somehow frivolous. The silence was becoming uncomfortable so John inquired politely to break the ice, "So what will happen to us now?" The prosecutor took a leisurely drag from his cigarette, and responded matter-of-factly, "You two are going to Jail".

Pat in his usual panic attack blurted out, "Jail! You mean we're really going to a real Jail?" Sensing Pat's distress, the prosecutor kindly reassured them, "Don't worry; it will be perhaps two or three years at the most." John sat in stunned silence. There was simply nothing more to say. This was really it! All hopes of getting out of this mess were gone - they were really heading to jail. No ifs, ands or buts about it.

As they were led outside the room, the chaotic mob tried to rush in past them again. This time, John and Pat were numb from the harsh reality they now faced. They hardly noticed the jostling of the unruly mob as they were led out to the waiting jeeps. The love fest was over.

Chapter 13

Tabriz Prison

On the road to prison that evening, John pondered the predicament they had gotten themselves into. He figured that dad was already mightily pissed at him for going to Iran against his will. When he hears about this, he's REALLY going to be pissed - and disappointed for sure. He could deal with dad's ire in time, but mom is going to be heartbroken and worried sick over this. He hated to think how hard she would take all this. He wished he could take it all back now. He remembered the postcard he wrote before leaving for Iran: "…Tell mom not to worry, I'll call when I get back in about a month." He was really eating those words now. He'd be lucky to get home in perhaps three or four years. He knew he had really let everyone down and there was nothing he could to do now to change that. He was on his way to prison.

John hadn't noticed that it had already gotten dark as the jeeps approached the gates to Tabriz prison. The prison was located at the outskirts of town. Upon first seeing the prison, John mistook it for some kind of a casino. In a bizarre scene reminiscent of "Apocalypse Now", there were bright Christmas lights strung everywhere in a macabre, but festive décor. The meaning of this odd juxtaposition was totally lost on John, maybe it was some kind of Islamic holiday decoration, but at this moment he really couldn't care less. This place was going to be his new home for quite some time to come. As the large metal gates swung open before him, he resigned himself to the fact that it would be a long time before he would see the outside world again.

****

Inside the prison, the newly arrived prisoners were unloaded and handed over to the prison guards for processing. It was apparent to John that the atmosphere here was a lot more serious than at police headquarters. The prison guards here were regular Iranian army soldiers, all well-armed with machine guns. John and Pat were led into the processing area where they were ordered to disrobe to their underwear. They turned over all of their belongings for inventory and safekeeping. They were issued their prison uniforms and told to put them on. They were real prisoners now and John regretted all that joking around about being international criminals. He felt stupid that he had even said those things.

The inner doors were unlocked and they were led off to their prison cells. This is De'ja' Vu, thought John as he recalled a scene from the movie, Midnight Express.

Midnight Express was based on the true story of Billy Hayes, a young American arrested for drug smuggling and sentenced to twenty years in a hellish Turkish prison. While in prison, Billy was subjected to repeated beatings and rape from a sadistic prison guard. In the end, Billy finally managed to escape from prison by killing his torturer and taking the "Midnight Express" to freedom.

As John walked down the dimly lit corridor, the irony of the thought was almost amusing except this wasn't some movie he was watching. This was for real. It was hard to believe just two days ago, they were planning on bragging about their adventures to their pals back in Munich. Now, he was headed for what might potentially be the worst experience of his life. John was by nature a survivor. He had always had a tough hide and he had a matter-of-fact way of dealing with adversity. He wasn't one to fret or waste time worrying about things he couldn't control. He would deal with this predicament as well.

****

In contrast to the notorious brutality of Turkish prisons, the Iranian prisons were known to be somewhat more humane. When they arrived at their assigned cells, John was grateful that his worst fears were not realized. Due to the white-collar nature of their crime as well as their status as foreign prisoners, John and Pat were taken to the prison's hospital wing for incarceration. Aside from those inmates who obviously needed medical attention, this wing of the prison was used to hold mainly foreigners and political prisoners. Luckily, the violent criminals were all kept permanently separated in the main section of the prison. At least he wouldn't have to sleep with his back to the wall and one eye open all the time. Compared to the rest of the prison, the conditions in the hospital wing were downright luxurious. The cells here were less crowded, much cleaner and the beds actually had sheets on them. Even the bathroom facilities were kept reasonably clean, thanks to the "lower class" prisoners who were sent over daily to clean the bathrooms. By all standards of prison life in the Middle East, they were extremely fortunate.

Upon entering their cells, John and Pat were pleasantly surprised to discover that their cellmates included two Americans, Steve and Tom. Knowing that they were not alone in this predicament was comforting in a way. Steve and Tom had both been arrested several months earlier on the very same charges that brought John and Pat there.

Steve had been a drifter wandering the world – he had spent time in Mexico, South America and Europe. He often took odd jobs along the way to support himself and his lifestyle. Tom was an expatriate American who normally resided in Canada. He was wandering through parts of Europe when he decided a diversion to the Middle East would be more interesting - an admittedly bad choice as it turned out.

As the veteran prisoners of the ward, Tom and Steve briefed the newcomers on protocol and what to expect in their new home. For starters, as Americans they could expect to be treated very well. They suggested the easiest way of befriending the guards was to teach them a little English each day. Ironically, although much of the Iranian populace publicly called for death to America, it seemed a significant majority of Iranians secretly harbored a desire to go live in America. Apparently many of them felt that being friendly with Americans and learning a few words of English would somehow help them get there faster. A rather hopeful assumption, Tom mused, but the mutual arrangement worked just fine for the American inmates. The guards often traded cigarettes and snacks for short lessons in return and everyone was happy.

Regarding matters of prison cuisine, Tom and Steve rated the chow as actually tolerable once you got used to it – lots of rice, some vegetables and a little meat or fish now and then. Certainly nothing to drool over, but it was a hard sight better than the swill often served to the hard core criminals. Overall, the accommodations here were adequate and comfortable. However as in all prisons, boredom and more boredom would become a constant companion. Tom and Steve warned that they should expect to do a lot of reading and spend many long hours playing chess and cards. More so than just physical incarceration, prison was a mind game.

Chapter 14

Settling In

A few days later, the local American consul came by to pay a visit to the two newly incarcerated inmates. The consul, Michael Metrinko, welcomed the pair to Tabriz prison and informed the pair that their parents have been contacted back home. They now knew where they were and have been notified of their current legal status as prisoners in pretrial detention. John felt some relief that his folks were at least aware of what happened to him.

Metrinko advised John and Pat of how best to proceed in their predicament. He suggested that it would be prudent to retain a local lawyer, Mr. G.H. Ipakchian, to represent them. Mr. Ipakchian had represented several similar cases so he was the choice pick for their case. Hiring a lawyer sooner than later would help them get a court date faster, and very likely a reduced sentence. If they were fine with that, he would send a message to their parents to wire the money via the consulate.

That sounded like prudent advice until they were told the lawyer's retainer fee would be one thousand dollars! At first, John was taken aback and hesitant. A thousand dollars was a large amount of money for our parents in those days. Dad was a junior grade civil servant struggling to raise three kids on his modest salary and that kind of money was hard to come by. After all, if John hadn't disobeyed his parents in the first place, he wouldn't be in this mess. How could he even ask them for such money? John didn't mind taking his punishment for what he had done, but he was loath to further punish his parents financially in the process.

At first, John asked Metrinko to let him sleep on it for a couple of days. He had a lot of thinking to do yet. But the more he thought about it, the serious reality of the situation dictated that he had no real choice but to follow the Consul's recommendation. The important thing for him was to get out of this situation as soon as possible. John decided that when he returned home he would get a job and repay the money to his parents. That evening, John sat down and reluctantly wrote an apologetic letter to his dad asking for the funds to be wired.

****

In the coming days and weeks, John and Pat acclimated to their new environment and settled into the routine of prison life. With plenty of time to spare, they got to know quite well some of the other prisoners who shared their ward. Each had their own story of how they got where they were: Agir, the Kurd was quite likeable and well educated as he spoke fluent French and passable English. He had been a leader of a Kurdish splinter group that had attempted to revolt against the Shah. He had lived in the part of western Iran that the Kurds considered to be part of their ancestral Kurdistan. The Kurds wanted autonomy from Iran and some like Agir were ready to press the issue through violent revolt. The revolution didn't get far as Agir was caught smuggling in arms from Turkey. As a result, he'd now been in prison now for eight years of his twenty-year sentence.

In the cell nearby was Hans, an Austrian truck driver who

had had the bad luck of having a serious vehicle accident in Iran. Hans was a pretty cool character with level temperament. He had a university education but instead found that the life of a truck driver resonated better with him. He played a good game of chess and was always up for any kind of card game. According to Hans, the only reason he was being held in prison was because the insurance company had so far refused to pay damages to the other party. Like insurance companies everywhere, they were taking their sweet time coming up with the settlement money. Four months after his accident, Hans was still waiting.

John learned that the entire upper floor above them was reserved for just two Iranian Army officers. One of them was a former Army general who got caught running drugs from Afghanistan. The general liked to keep to himself and rarely mingled with anyone else. On the other hand, his fellow inmate was a rather amiable Colonel named Ibrahim who spoke very good English. Colonel Ibrahim's crime was that he was none too happy with some of the Shah's policies, and the Shah in turn was none too happy with him. He dared to protest too much and one day the Shah answered by putting him away for being politically incorrect.

In his often long talks with John, he explained that the Shah's days in power were numbered and that a revolution was coming. According to Ibrahim, the Shah had done much to modernize Iran and raised the standard of living substantially during his reign. However he warned that there had been a long stewing resentment with the Shah's overtly pro-western politics – especially among the mullahs. The Shah often reacted with heavy-handed excesses to protect his regime. He was ready and willing to leverage his feared and brutal secret police, the Savak, to maintain control in his land. The Colonel's words were foreboding, but John found it hard to believe that the powerful Shah could be deposed anytime soon. In due time, John would come to realize that the Colonel's words would ring true a lot sooner than anyone had imagined at the time.

****

One week later, the party became a bit merrier as yet another new group of car runners were busted and brought to Tabriz prison. This new group came from a variety of countries and included a few rather eccentric characters: Adolf was a balding, short, bearded Austrian who was heavily into Buddism and meditation. Brendon, 29 years old, was a gregarious Australian that was addicted to telling stupid jokes.

Adolf was actually great. He was docile and quiet and he liked to keep to himself most of the time meditating for extended periods in his cell. When he wasn't meditating, he would spend hours reading his little book of Buddhism. When he finished reading the book, he would go right back to the beginning and start all over again. He seemed not to mind at all being in prison. In fact he seemed to welcome the experience and took to incarceration in jail as would a monk to a stint in a monastery. He explained to the others that although his body was in prison, his mind was free to roam the universe. Thus, he could never be imprisoned in the same way as the others perceived their condition. At least Adolf was harmless, even if a little odd. The rest of the group pretty much left him alone to do his thing.

Brendon, aka "Big Ben" was an Australian with a German mother who lived down under. Ben was a truck driver by profession who had spent most of his life driving trucks in South Africa and Rhodesia, as it was known then. He sported a big beer belly, but that wasn't necessarily the result from drinking too much beer.

Most of it was actually caused by wounds he suffered when he hit a land mine in Rhodesia. Some of the shrapnel severed stomach muscles and causing a permanent sag in his abdomen. In typical Aussie style, Ben was burly and gregarious. Everyone enjoyed his company and listening to his stories from Africa. Ben's only downside was that he had a repertoire of stale and corny jokes that got old real quick. Aside from that, he was pretty cool.

Chapter 15
New Mates New Troubles

The ranks of the newly "busted" car runners just kept on growing. Shortly after Adolph and Brendon joined the group, several more new arrivals were brought to the prison. There were a couple more Germans in the latest group. One was Reinhardt he turned out to be quite the opposite of Adolf.

Weighing in at a mere hundred pounds or so, Rheinhardt's entire body was covered in tattoos. He insisted on being called "Ricco" for some reason and was boisterous and belligerent from the moment he arrived. Ricco had a real chip on his shoulder and he warned that nobody better mess with him. Sensing Ricco's insecurity, the others quickly reassured him that no one in the ward was going to give him a hard time. It was safe there and he had nothing to worry about.

It quickly became apparent to everyone that Ricco was a lot more than just insecure. In fact he was a real bona fide nutcase. He couldn't speak any English, but he would always jabber away in German at anyone who happened to be nearby. Mostly it was about how he had pummeled or stabbed people who had offended or cheated him. He would constantly extrapolate his prior actions into future threats of harm on anyone who would dare to do the same to him again. John and Pat came to regret the day that they let Ricco know that they could both speak some German.

After a few days of this, everyone decided to simply ignore Ricco's senseless ranting and threats. Offended by the brush-off and cold shoulders from his cellmates, he then took to chastising and ranting at the guards for one thing or another. This not only angered the guards, but the other inmates as well. Ricco was becoming a real threat to the harmonious relationship they had built up with the guards. Pretty soon, everyone started yelling at Ricco to "shut your ass up, Ricco" every time he would go mouthing off to a guard. Failing that, they took to throwing cups, pillows, sandals and other small items at him to shut him up. Steve even suggested that they might have to tie up Ricco and gag him if it came to that. Unfortunately, all this only served to set him off even more. Ricco was a nutcase all right.

The second German in the new group was Bernhardt. Bernhardt was the quiet and studious type who spent much of his time reading. He stayed mostly to himself and the others left him alone unless he felt unusually sociable. Everyone thanked God that Bernhardt wasn't like Ricco and that was reason enough to like him.

****

For John and Pat, the days soon melted into weeks, and weeks became months. Daily prison life quickly became routine and largely uneventful; overall it was a tolerable existence. John made good use of his time in jail. For starters, he began learning how to play the harmonica. In fact John had always been musically inclined as he had played the clarinet throughout middle school and high school. He also started getting fairly regular German lessons from Steve who spoke excellent German. He was determined to come out of jail a better person than went in.

The highlight of John's existence, as is most any inmate's, was the letters and the packages from home. On October 22nd, 1978, my dad wrote:

Dear John,

I have sent Mr. Metrinko $1,200 on this date for your defense and personal expenses ($50 monthly). We borrowed it from Tom rather than dig into the credit union at this time. Please use it wisely.

We have not received any more mail from you since your letter of 12 Sep and mine of 1 Oct. So, since there aren't any questions to your answer, I only have a few to ask. We sent you an English style army sweater in one of the packages, but you have not acknowledged receipt. Did they let you have it? Have you had any new additions to your little group?

Tom received your letter the other day (The one you wrote on 18 Sep and could not send until 9 Oct or so). We all got a few laughs out of it and commented that the heap you drove must have really been a wreck on arrival. It's a wonder you made it all.

Did you receive the packages we sent on 5 Oct yet? The contents were as follows: Long Underwear, socks, coffee, Peanut butter, tobacco, garlic powder, cremora, kimchi, mustard, soy sauce, soup, sugar, swiss miss, snack pack, sardines, spam corn chips, shampoo, cookies, kool aid, potato chips, beef jerky and strawberry jam.

Please write soon (I also sent a book of stamps to Mr. Metrinko for you) and let us know how you are proceeding with your lawyer, on

your defense etc., and how you are doing.
    Love, Dad.

In October, Pat's parents, Colonel Tiahrt and his wife, came to visit us at our home in Nieder Weisel. The meeting helped ease the shared pain that both of our families were going through. It also gave us a chance to compare notes, letters and strategies as to what, if anything could be done. Not only were both parents interested in freeing their sons, they were equally interested in helping to put the car runners out of business. The last thing they wanted to see were more young kids getting sucked into this mess. To facilitate the process, dad enlisted the assistance of Herr Hans-Eberhard Hoffman who was the local police chief in Butzbach and a good friend of our family. He generously helped us to get investigations opened by both the German CID and Interpol.

The Tiahrts were also interested in hearing John's letters. John was very good about writing and keeping us informed. John wrote often and in good detail. By comparison, Pat's letters home were infrequent, short and vague. The Tiahrts listened intently as we read them John's latest letter dated October 11th:

Dear Mom & Dad,

I received your letter of 1 Oct today, and with it the package containing the sweater, shirt and munchies. Thanks much, the sweater will come in handy as will the shirt.

Two days ago, Pat and I were taken to the city courthouse to the office of the prosecutor. Our lawyer (Mr. Ipakchian) had asked that we be called in to complete our file. We were taken there on a police bus with 7 guards, one armed with a rifle. We were handcuffed and taken in to see the prosecutor. It seems in answering questions when we were first arrested, we were not aware of the technical nature in which our replies would be taken. For example, I wrote, "I did not intend to break any laws". Mr. Ipakchian told us this was bad, that we should change it to "I did not break any laws, somebody else did, and so on". It seems a lawyer is definitely essential. All in all, the interview wasn't bad. The prosecutor bought us cokes, gave me a pack of Dunhills, offered to allow us to go shopping in the city before we go back to the prison, etc.... All in all, they were very nice to us.

Things are definitely beginning to look up. With all of the killing and destruction going on in Iran, they seem to be sorry they arrested us. The consul says with much more serious crimes to contend with, we have turned out to be an excess load on the entire system. The prosecutor said that he is sympathetic toward us but since this is a Federal charge, he has no choice but to prosecute us. Which means there is a good chance he may recommend the minimum sentence for us. All things considered it seems I will be here less than a year, I hope so....

Take care, John

P.S. Pat's also doing well. He may be getting a bit sillier at that, but his main concern at all times is beer and women. He misses them terribly. It may be enough to drive him over the edge. Well, no big loss. Tell his parents he's never been better; completely sober for 3 months.

The last part got a big laugh from all of us.

****

In Tabriz prison, life ground on day by day for John and his cellmates. In addition to being allowed to shower on Thursdays and Sundays, the prison barber came around once a week to give haircuts to those who needed it. John and Pat always made it a point to tip the barber a few Rials which made the barber very happy.

They also devised ways to keep prison life interesting as possible; for example, they started picking dandelions from the prison courtyard to make dandelion wine. It wasn't the best tasting wine, but it was the closest thing to a real drink they had in months. More importantly, it gave them something constructive to occupy their time.

The regimen each day began with a couple of the day's "volunteers" going down to the mess building to fetch hot water and food for breakfast. The food was brought back to the ward in a big plastic bucket and the hot water was used to make tea and coffee. Compared to the pitifully small portions that the hardcore prisoners got down at the mess hall, everyone received hefty portions in the hospital ward. They weren't about to go hungry even if the chow wasn't the best.

When the food arrived, everyone lined up with their bowl and spoon in hand as the volunteers served the food. The menu was largely predictable, usually consisting of rice and corn, rice and beans or rice and pieces of fat. Meat was such a rarity that one day, Pat held up the bucket and facetiously declared; "This is our lucky day boys. We're dining on some fine rat meat tonight!" Indeed it was mystery meat, but nonetheless it was meat of some kind. That was better than no meat at all.

They also had privileged access to the prison store where they could purchase additional tins of food and snacks to supplement the bland prison food. Each person found creative ways to enhance the daily dish to their liking. John swore that there was nothing that a good dose of Tabasco sauce and soy sauce couldn't cure. Finally, the goodies that came in the CARE packages from home rounded out their meager diets with the occasional treat of chocolate and cookies.

****

Because they were minimum-security prisoners, they were free to wander the prison courtyard between the hours of 5am and 10pm. At night, the door to the hospital wing was locked, but the cells themselves were left open allowing access to the communal bathroom facilities. Everyone was truly grateful for this perk as the thought of otherwise having to smell everyone's piss and shit cans all night was not a pleasant alternative.

The guards assigned to watch over the hospital ward were by and large benign and friendly to the foreigners. They quickly figured out that Ricco was the only one they could expect trouble from so they made a point of locking him up separately as punishment. This of course made Ricco go ballistic but it sure made the rest of the group very happy.

Most of the guards assigned to the hospital wing were Army conscripts from small villages. On the whole, they were poorly educated and a few were even illiterate. The guards who could speak a little English eagerly struck up conversations with the Americans to improve their English and learn about America. At times, the difference between the publicly professed hate for America versus the privately professed desire to become an American citizen was amazing. It was just another one of the enigmatic facets of the Middle East. A friendly little chat and a cigarette now and then went a long way to keep the peace and to assure preferential treatment. In time, the atmosphere in the hospital ward became so cordial that sometimes the guards making their rounds would often help themselves to an empty bed and take a nice afternoon nap amongst the prisoners. As long as they kept Ricco locked up, everything was just fine in the hospital ward.

****

Located next door to the hospital ward was the looney ward. As a convenient way to keep the mentally disturbed warehoused; the prisons in Iran often served double duty as insane asylums. Aside from one inmate that hung himself in the bathroom prior to John's arrival, the loonies were mostly harmless and provided amusement to an otherwise dull prison life.

Crazy Hassan was one such inmate. No one knew how long he had been there, but as long as anybody could remember, he had been chained to his bed. Where ever Hassan went, so too went the bed. He dragged it with him everywhere, making a great big racket in the process. During his periodic bouts of frustration, he would often go over to the guard shack and slam his metal bed against the door. If the guards became annoyed enough, they would come out and beat him with rubber hoses and heavy electrical cables.

As if that weren't appalling enough, Hassan's piercing screams seemed to trigger a sadistic reflex in the general upstairs. When he heard the screams, the general would rush out to the guard shack with broom stick in hand and proceed to gleefully join in on the beating. Initially, the foreign inmates were shocked by this display of wonton cruelty, but it soon began to appear that Hassan actually enjoyed his regular beatings.

One particularly burly and brutal guard nicknamed "Orc" made a ritual of beating Hassan on the bottom of his feet. With each strike, Hassan would make short high-pitched howls like an injured dog, hobble around the courtyard and come back for more. John surmised that the beatings probably released some sort of chemical in Hassan's brain that actually made him feel better afterwards. Whatever the reason, the beatings became such commonplace that the foreigners started coming out to the courtyard with chairs and drinks in hand to watch the regular "show". It was entertaining in a macabre sort of way.

Another inmate of the looney ward was Karim. Karim was an Iranian national who had lived in California at one time and spoke excellent English. At first, he seemed to be rather charming and otherwise perfectly "normal". It wasn't too long however, before he began telling everyone that the agents of the International Red Cross were pursuing him. Not the CIA, not the KGB, but yes - the Red Cross!

This odd paranoia was rather amusing to everyone at first, but after a few weeks John began to notice a distinct change come over Karim. Karim started to become overtly paranoid about every little thing. He saw "evidence" everywhere of people conspiring against him. At times, he would refuse to eat claiming that the food was poisoned. About the same time, he stopped taking showers and refused to clean himself up in any way. The smell quickly reached offensive levels and everyone began to chide him to either take a shower or stay the hell away. Getting ostracized by the group only served to heighten his paranoia and he soon declared that they too were ALL agents of the International Red Cross. His regression continued to worsen until finally, he would sit in a corner all-day rocking back and forth while wallowing in his own filth. One day, the guards came and took him away. After that, John never saw him again.

Finally, there was "Popeye" the Turk, who went around wanting to attack and kill everyone. Tom had aptly nicknamed him

"Popeye" for his asymmetrical eyes somewhat akin to the popular cartoon character. "Popeye the Turk" was blind and squinty in one eye, but his good eye was his evil eye. It seemed overly large as if to make up for the bad eye and it had a most piercing and crazed look to it. He would often graphically talk about killing the guards by slitting their throats and escaping. Everyone learned to stay clear of him as they sensed he was very unpredictable and volatile. Their hunches were well founded; they discovered that the strange noise they heard late at night was Popeye crafting a crude knife from a piece of metal. Thankfully, one day the guards came and took Popeye away before he could cause any serious mayhem. Rumor had it that they took him over to section six where they kept the hardcore criminals.

Chapter 16
The Gathering Storm

Although imprisonment is never a desirable situation, life in Tabriz prison was not nearly as bad as anyone had initially feared. Even if they had to serve out their full two to three year sentences, it would certainly be tolerable under the present circumstances. There had also been some encouraging words recently heard on the grapevine; a New Zealander serving time on the same charges at another prison had been released after serving just nine months. To John, Pat and the others, things were beginning to look up a bit with each passing day.

Outside of the prison walls however, the political landscape was rapidly deteriorating on a daily basis. The ominous undercurrent of a revolution that Ibrahim warned about was beginning to spread rapidly across the nation of Iran. In recent months, the long suppressed rumblings of dissent had erupted into dozens of large-scale demonstrations led by fundamentalist Islamic students and clergy. Despite the government's strong arm tactics, the demonstrations were rapidly gaining momentum and spreading to the smaller cities outside of Tehran. Already, many hundreds were dead and more were dying almost every day. The violence was spreading rapidly.

Since coming to power in 1925, the rule of the Pahlavi dynasty over the nation of Iran had been absolute. To the Western powers, Reza Pahlavi was considered an unusually progressive Middle Eastern ruler for his liberal interpretation of Islam and ready acceptance of western ways. America especially appreciated a strong pro-Western ally in this part of the world. With the steady stream of revenue coming from the oilfields, the Shah had modernized and westernized Iran into one of the most progressive countries of the Middle East. On the surface, Iran appeared to be the model of what an oil-rich Middle-Eastern nation could become. However, the Shah's vision and polices were not embraced by everyone, nor had the prosperity touched all levels of Iranian society. The Shah's willing embrace of western values and culture had for years offended the hard-line Islamic clerics inside Iran. Those who protested the Shah's policies were often brutally repressed by "Savak", the Shah's secret police force. In the course of these events, the United States with its military and political support came to symbolize the dominant evil that made it possible for the Shah to sustain his iron grip over the Iranian people.

One particularly vocal cleric living in exile in Paris challenged the Shah's power directly by calling for the establishment of an Islamic state in Iran. That cleric was the Ayatollah Khomeini. Khomeini saw the Shah as a mere puppet of the United States and called for his overthrow. His angry declarations touched the cord of many disenfranchised Iranians and the momentum of dissent began to spread like wildfire across Iran. In the spring of 1978, the first images of angry mobs chanting "down with the Shah" and "death to America" began to flicker across the TV sets around the world. At that time, few believed that one of the most stable and modern countries in the Middle East could be overthrown by a radical fundamentalist cleric exiled in France. In less than a year however, the Iranian revolution would explode in its full fury and unleash its terrible rage against America. Trapped squarely in the eye of this gathering storm was John, Pat and their small group of foreign inmates. They were completely helpless to escape the gathering storm outside the prison walls. All they could do was monitor the developments on the daily shortwave news broadcast on BBC.

****

As fall turned into winter, the weather grew colder and the days shorter. By early November, heavy snow blanketed Tabriz and the surrounding region. In just the few months since their arrest, the prison itself had become an unexpected sanctuary from the troubles outside, but time was running out. There was nothing the prisoners could do except live life day to day; they were trapped and powerless to do anything about it.

It was difficult to predict how the political changes outside of the prision walls would affect them. If the Shah's government fell, then the prison would simply come under new management. If it came to that, the new management would probably not be as kind and accommodating to the foreigners, especially the Americans – or they just might be happy to kick out the trouble-making Yanks with the other riffraff westerners. If that were to be the case, everybody hoped the regime change would come sooner than later. Honestly, it was anybody's guess as to what would actually happen when the time came. John decided not to worry about things he had no control over.

The Americans especially looked forward to the visits by the Consul. These visits were a chance to catch up on the news, ask questions, exchange mail and receive CARE packages from home. Lately though, the consul had other more pressing matters that required his attention and the visits became less frequent and haphazard. On December 10th, 1978 a massive demonstration of an estimated 100,000 marched past the consulate in Tabriz chanting "Death to America". Metrinko was offered a helicopter to evacuate, but he chose to stay put. Luckily, this time there was no serious violence and the crowds dispersed after a time.

Sometimes, the missionaries from the local Evangelical church came by to check in on the welfare of the foreigners. Several times, reverend Meloy himself had come to see how they were doing and offer spiritual guidance for those prisoners who wanted it. They brought with them books, magazines and English language newspapers that helped to keep them informed of the outside world. John and Pat weren't church-going types by any stretch of the imagination, but the friendly reverend's visits helped boost morale. It was nice of him to come by even if for a little chat.

One day, they even received a surprise visit from some fellow students from the University of Maryland. John and Pat had earlier sent the university a letter warning other students of their plight and asking for any assistance they could give. They didn't seriously expect much to come of it, as John and Pat weren't exactly the Dean's favorite students. Nonetheless, it was very thoughtful of Dean McMahon to urge some students on their way to India to stop by and pay a visit to their incarcerated schoolmates. They brought with them some recent magazines and the latest gossip from around school. It was a most welcomed break from the daily routine.

Due to the political troubles brewing on the outside, the dates for John and Pat's preliminary court hearing kept getting pushed out on a regular basis. As time went on, the courts around Iran started to feel the sting of the anti-government demonstrations and were often closed for many days at a time. The prosecutors suddenly had much more to worry about than spending time investigating the petty cases of some car-running foreign boys. If anything, things were coming to such a head that many of the officials would have been just as happy to send the foreigners home.

****

That Christmas, we had little to be merry about back home. The news from Iran became worse with each passing day. In a strange way, we were now glad that John was in prison as it was one of the few safe places left in Iran for Americans. We could only hope that the New Year would bring John's release.

Far away in Iran, Our Christmas CARE package to John luckily arrived a few days before Christmas. On Christmas Eve, John wrote:

"Well its Christmas Eve today and by pooling everyone's food we had a little party (with a bit of home made wine). Not a bad Christmas Eve actually. All the Iranis are greeting us with "Merry Christmas", though they're not exactly sure what it's all about. They're all pretty happy since it seems that the Shah has announced that everybody will either be amnestied or get a reduction in sentence after the New Year (which is March 21st for them). So we're having a tolerable Christmas, hope you all have a good Christmas and a New Year."

-John

A few days later, the New Year arrived and gave us renewed hope. We raised our glasses to toast John's homecoming that year. Likewise, in Tabriz, John and his pals raised their tin cups of dandelion wine and cheerfully toasted 1979 as "the year we go home!"

Chapter 17
Unwanted Guests

The little kerosene stove in the center of the common area was already lit, but the ward was still chilly from the cold clear night. It was one of those winter mornings where John just wanted to stay put in bed until breakfast came. It had seemed like a good plan until John's fitful slumber was disturbed by some loud commotion coming from the mess hall outside. A few other heads were already raised in muted alarm when John opened his eyes.

Ben was already standing at one of the windows watching. "Some shit's happening over there."

The cacophony of excited voices outside kept growing louder. Apparently something was going down over at the mess hall. The prisoners of the hospital ward wrapped their blankets around them and gathered at the windows. Below them, they saw excited guards come pouring out of the guard shack and make their way to the adjoining compound. They were decked out in riot gear; clubs, shields and face masks at the ready. The guards fired tear gas rounds into the mess building and in short order, the noisy ruckus was quelled as dazed, coughing prisoners began stumbling outside. Eventually a couple dozen of them were corralled in front of the mess hall where they received first aid.

Everyone speculated it must have been a riot or a fight of some sort. Now that calm was restored, John walked out to the courtyard and flagged a guard to find out what happened. He returned a minute later to share the scuttlebutt with his cellmates; according to the guard, a group of Turks and Persians who had been insulting each other had finally had enough of each other. Ignited by age-old ethnic hatreds, a fight broke out which soon deteriorated into a general melee in the mess hall. It appeared now that everything was back under control and there was nothing more to worry about. In fact everyone's primary concern now was that their breakfast might be delayed this morning due to the fight.

****

It wasn't but ten or fifteen minutes later that the group of Persians who were injured in the fighting was brought into the hospital ward for treatment. No one seemed to know where the injured Turks were taken, but the guards made sure they were kept separate to avoid any further problems. To the dismay of the residents of the hospital ward, these new arrivals were mostly unsavory hard-core criminal types. Most of them were already serving serious sentences for some sort of violent crime. These were the Hard Core Lifers! They were all obnoxious, smelly and dirty. The previously safe and calm haven of the hospital ward was rudely invaded by vermin filth. Suddenly, life became very unpleasant here. The foreigners found themselves having to share the ward with sixteen mean and nasty troublemakers. Things were not looking good for the foreign contingent and they hoped the presence of the Hard Core dregs would be very temporary.

Everyone's worst fears were realized that very first night. No sooner had they locked the ward for the night, the Hard Cores got to work and began tearing the ward apart! Everyone watched with nervous apprehension as the goons started stripping pieces of aluminum from various bathroom fixtures and metal furniture and began sharpening them into makeshift knives and spears. As foreigners watched from their cells, they wondered if those weapons might be turned against them. Perhaps they planned to take the foreigners as hostages? That thought had crossed their minds.

Luckily, the foreigners were spared being used as hostages, but the next three weeks became sheer misery. From morning till night, the Hard Cores constantly argued amongst themselves in loud belligerent voices. Just about any little thing seemed to set them off in a contested yelling and shoving match. If one of them was so much as seen talking to a foreigner, the others suddenly became jealous and fought for equal attention. Not only were these goons annoying as hell, but were also totally gross; spit flew from their mouths incessantly as they yakked all day.

Simple activities such as reading and chess became almost impossible – in fact virtually all of the Hard Cores were illiterate so the act of even reading was a curiosity magnet that drew their unwanted attention. Just about anything the foreigners did, attracted the Hard Cores like flies: card games, writing letters, even doing push-ups. It was miserable; no one wanted the goons near them, but giving one the cold shoulder could get you stabbed or killed! Everyone prayed that the Hard Cores would be shipped back to whence they came much sooner than later. Nothing good could come of their continued presence in the hospital ward.

****

One night in early January, the Hard Cores decided to cook up some serious trouble. They had seemed unusually quiet that evening. Instead of the usual bellicose yelling matches, they were speaking more in hushed tones. The quiet respite was a welcome change, but this wasn't normal behavior for them. John confided to Pat and the others that he had a hunch these guys they were up to no good. His hunch was confirmed shortly thereafter when one of them came around the ward telling the foreigners to get back into their cells.

Omar, the bearded wiry one that spoke a little English gestured for everyone to head towards their cells and go to sleep, he kept repeating "Everybody inside now, e'sleep now...e'snake coming..."

Apparently, "E'snake coming" was their secret code that things were going down tonight. Sensing the impending trouble, everyone made haste back to their cells. When all of the foreigners had retreated to their cells, one of the Hard Cores picked up a chair and sent it crashing through a nearby window. Several others simultaneously jumped the startled guards, grabbing their firearms. Totally caught by surprise, the two guards panicked and fled for the safety of the guard shack screaming for help.

In quick succession, three more windows were smashed out and tables overturned. Then in some sort of a bizarre ritual, the Hard Cores then began cutting into their own scalps with their knives. Apparently they believed the bleeding made them look more menacing to the guards. Screaming and yelling, they poured out of the ward with captured guns, metal rods, home made knives and even chairs. They made their way across the courtyard and then started attacking the guard shack, smashing the windows trying to break down the security door. The foreigners rushed to the broken windows to watch the action unfolding across the courtyard.

Beyond the guard shack, they could see a riot squad forming once again to engage the Hard Cores with shields, clubs and tear gas launchers. Obviously, these goons didn't know when to quit! John yelled for everyone to grab towels and wet them in case they fired the tear gas canisters into the courtyard. With the windows busted out, they could get a nasty dose of the fumes themselves.

The situation was growing very tense and after about ten minutes, the warden finally came out to confront the violent mob. The warden threw cartons of cigarettes out to the Hard Cores and they quickly calmed down. Apparently, this whole stupid revolt was about insufficient cigarette rations...or something like that. With cigarettes in hand, the Hard Cores soon returned to their cells peacefully. But thanks to their senseless vandalism, it was now colder than hell in the Ward. Everyone froze their butts until they got the windows boarded up.

****

Having had witnessed the volatility of the Hard Core bunch, John and the others tried to stay out of the way of the Hard Cores as much as possible. Everyone smiled at them a lot and engaged in polite conversation if the Hard Cores felt a need to be especially sociable. Mostly though, the hard cores weren't interested in conversation as such; instead they had a compulsive need to get in your face and talk on and on about how they were going to attempt another break out again soon.

For the westerners who valued their personal space, this was a most uncomfortable experience. The Hard Cores would sit down next to them and lean in real close, sometimes just inches from their faces. The sight of their rotting teeth and bad breath up close and personal was a hideous experience. Of course no one dared offend them by moving away in disgust. All they could do was to politely endure this assault on the senses while the Hard Cores shared their plans of how they would make their next move.

They revealed that their plan was to wait until they were ordered moved to another prison. Along the way, they planned to kill their guards with knives and make their escape into the mountains. Perhaps they were hoping that some of the foreigners would be interested in joining them in the mountains as fugitives. Who knew? Whatever their motive for wanting to share their secrets, these guys were a crazy bunch. No one knew for sure if these guys might turn on them one day. Everyone was always on edge as long as these nuts were hanging around.

One day in late January, every one's prayers were finally answered. That afternoon, a large group of well-armed guards came into the ward and told the Hard Cores it was time to move out. As the Hard Cores shuffled out in handcuffs and leg chains, the foreigners bid them a fond farewell. When the last of them had left and the doors closed behind them, there was a sudden sense of peace and relief they hadn't known in some time. The Hard Cores were gone! They were really gone!

"Well, the bitches are gone" said Steve.

John looked at the others, "So what the hell are we waiting for? Let's partyyyy!!!"

Everyone cheered as Pat broke out the Dandelion wine and within minutes, the remaining supply was exhausted. Even normally docile Adolph joined in the celebration. Why, this was the next best thing to getting released! The foreigners had their ward back and it seemed that life in the hospital ward would at last return to normal.

Chapter 18
The Ayatollah Returns

On January 16th, 1979 word came down that the Shah had left Iran for an undetermined period. At the controls of his personal Boeing 707, the Shah and his immediate family departed Iran for what would be the last time. The official reason given for the trip was that he and the empress were going abroad for a rest. In his stead, he left the Prime Minister, Dr. Shahpur Bakhtiar in charge of the government. Despite the official line, the conventional wisdom on the street was that the Shah was running for his life.

Beyond the prison walls nothing was normal in Iran anymore. Chaos was beginning to well up everywhere with massive rioting and violent demonstrations becoming almost a daily occurrence. That day, thousands gathered outside Tabriz prison demanding the release of all prisoners. A swift response with tear gas and shots fired into the air broke up the demonstration but total revolution was becoming imminent as elements of the military began to show signs of a split in allegiance.

****

Back in Germany, our family anxiously watched the rapidly evolving news events each night. The entire country of Iran seemed to thirst for American blood and there was my brother - caught right smack in the middle of the raging storm. As the images of the tumultuous events swept across the TV screens, we were totally helpless to do anything more. We speculated on what all of this would mean to John and his mates. With state authority collapsing around them, would they simply be forgotten there? Would the revolutionaries come and hang the evil westerners as they publicly preach? Or would they be taken hostage to extract demands of America?

To make matters worse, the postal system along with virtually all government services in Iran were beginning to grind to a halt. Letters that used to take roughly ten days to reach their destination was now taking more than a month. Even the APO (Army Post Office) postal system which the consulate used was affected adversely with backed up mail.

Despite the furious hatred unleashed against America, the prison guards remarkably continued to treat their captives just as they had before. The relations were still friendly and none of them showed any signs of hostility against the foreigners. Towards the end of January though, the foreigners could sense a distinct unease settling in amongst the higher ranking officers. In particular, the warden looked especially grim. Their tension was evident as they spent a lot of time hunched over the radio. They had good reason to be nervous. As officers of the national army, their allegiance could come into question any moment. Who would they support? Would they support the Shah's loyalists, or side with the Islamic revolutionaries? The wrong answer to either authority might result in their imprisonment or worse yet, summary execution. A few of the guards expecting the Shah to never return openly started wearing white armbands to show solidarity with the revolutionaries.

This was a bold move on their part, but it underscored the rapidly waning support for the Shah. Understandably, the guards had much on their minds these days.

****

On February 1st, 1979, the event many Iranians had waited for finally arrived; the Alyatollah Khomeni had returned to Iran from Paris. With the Shah already in absentia, millions of Iranians turned out to welcome the defiant cleric home. Upon arrival, the Ayatollah Khomeni made no attempt to hide his intentions. In a direct challenge to power of the existing regime, he declared openly that he would "Smash in the mouth of the Bakhtiar government." The gauntlet had been laid down and the end of Prime Minister Bahktiar's fragile government was assured.

The Police and the military looked to their senior leadership for direction. Over the next ten days, the situation was extremely tense. Military leaders and politicians scrambled to prevent a total meltdown of Iranian society. Many hundreds had already died over the past months in violent anti-government demonstrations and the now they were on the verge of total revolution. By February the 8th, entire units and bases began to mutiny against the Bahktiar government. Subsequently, armories were looted and a showdown of power was at hand. The senior military leadership already loathe to spill anymore blood of their citizens finally announced on February 11th that they would declare neutrality in the confrontation between the government and the people. With this calculated move by the military, The Bahktiar government effectively lost all power and authority. On hearing this announcement, a general uprising swept across Iran bringing an end to the Pahlavi Dynasty.

****

February 12th, 1979. The weather had suddenly turned warmer and the sun shone brightly on this beautiful February morning. By noon, John decided it had warmed up enough to go out to the courtyard and catch some sun for a while. It seemed to be the perfect day for a little R&R. He grabbed his blanket and his portable radio and walked out to the courtyard for a nice relaxing nap. John made him self comfortable in the warm afternoon sun and turned on his radio. Oddly, the daily English language news program he always listened to did not come on as scheduled this day. John thought perhaps someone had messed with the tuning dial but that was not the case. The station came in just where it was supposed to be on the dial. Instead of the news, the station just kept on playing Iranian martial music.

Puzzled, John tried two other stations known to carry English language news programs but he just got more of the same. As he scanned the radio band, every single station on the air simply blared out more martial music. Was this some sort of military holiday he didn't know about? John left the radio on his usual station hoping the news program would break in any minute. In an utterly bizarre twist, the station went so far as to play "Stars and Stripes forever" in its mix. John finally turned the radio off and relaxed in the quiet afternoon sun.

John's quiet nap was interrupted when several fighter jets came screaming in low over the city jarring him awake with a deafening roar. No sooner had the roar of the jets subsided, a gaggle of military helicopters added to the din. John was mighty annoyed that his peaceful afternoon in the sun was ruined, and the ruckus seemed definitely out of the ordinary. Between all of the martial music, the jets and the helicopters, it sure seemed like it was some big military holiday in progress. As the noise of the planes and the helicopters abated in the distance, John laid back hoping there would be no more interruptions. He closed his eyes to resume his rest. Thank goodness, the skies were quiet again.

It wasn't five minutes later that his peace was again interrupted. This time it wasn't low-flying aircraft, but instead he could now hear the sound of chanting voices. John sat up to listen; it was drifting over the walls from Section Six. Now, John's internal antenna kicked in and began to sense that something was amiss here. Hell, this was no holiday! The martial music must have been some sort of signal! John stood up in the court yard to make out what they were saying. The defiant chorus was building now and he could clearly make out the words; *"Khomeini e imam, Khomeini e imam…"*

The chanting had alerted the others and they joined John in the courtyard to wait and watch in anticipation. One of the guards wearing the white armband came up to the foreigners with a raised fist and a great big smile. *"Bakhtiar is no more! The Shah is finished! Khomeini is our leader! We are very happy!"*

So that was it! Khomeini had begun the showdown! There was a big change in management under way and the revolution would now kick into full force. Understandably, the prison population was almost without exception staunchly pro-Khomeini. After all, it was the Shah's government and his laws that had put them there. For many of the prisoners, Khomeini's return meant certain amnesty. For the rest, the collapse of civil government simply meant anarchy and a chance to make a break for freedom.

John and the others understood the stage was now set

for something big to happen. As the afternoon dragged on, the chanting became louder and louder accentuated with banging thousands of metal bowls and cups. Everyone was on edge but they were powerless to do anything. All they could do was to bring their chairs out into the sunshine and sip some Dandelion wine and wait. The big show was on.

****

Around three o'clock in the afternoon, plumes of smoke began to rise up out of the other sections of the prison. John and the others surmised that the prisoners must have set their mattresses on fire. Things were literally getting hot now! In the middle of the courtyard, everyone stood on their toes and chairs to get a better look over the walls. Steve thought he had seen some prisoners getting outside of their secured areas and onto the roof. Seconds later, a burst of machine gun fire erupted from one of the guard towers and everyone dropped to the ground. Another burst followed, and then another. With hearts pounding and a sudden rush of adrenalin, John and the others went dashing back into the safety of the hospital ward. Within moments, the other heavy machine guns on the guard towers joined in and opened up. The adjacent compound was being raked back and forth with deadly fire. Intermixed were sounds of shotgun blasts and the whump, whump of teargas canisters.

Back inside, John instinctively took cover under his bed. Aside from a couple of stray rounds knocking out a few panes from the windows, all of the firing was so far directed at the other parts of the prison. But all that could change in a split second; the hospital wing was no longer any kind of sanctuary. Trapped with no place to go, it seemed to John that this might be the last minutes of his life. Maybe he'd get hit by a bullet, or the fire would spread to their wing and burn them alive, or perhaps an angry mob would lynch them just because they were foreign devils. Sure as hell, there were a lot of threats out there that could end his life that night. Unable to do much else, John grabbed his notepad and began to write furiously, *"Here I am, hiding under my bed. Outside, all hell is breaking loose…"*

As bullets periodically ricocheted off the walls, the firing and the chanting continued outside. After a while, John and the others became numb to the mayhem and human curiosity took over. They cautiously crawled over to the back windows to get a better view of the situation outside. They caught a glimpse of a guard in the nearest tower furiously firing his heavy machine gun into the adjoining compound. They watched and waited as an hour passed, then two and then three hours. Planning their next move seemed futile, they were totally at the mercy of events. The revolutionary forces unleashed this day were sure to consume them one way or another. Each person coped in their own way. Adolph as usual sought solace in his book of Buddhism. Pat was chain smoking every cigarette in sight. John stayed focused on chronicling the events that would probably lead to his demise. Many sat quietly absorbed in their private thoughts, wondering if there was any chance in hell that they could survive this dilemma.

****

The din of battle outside remained constant as the sun set and darkness settled. In the darkness, the flames from the burning prison lit up the night with an eerie orange glow. By now, large sections of the prison were burning fiercely out of control. Strangely, the firing that had gone on unabated for over three hours now came to an abrupt halt. Moments later, a thunderous roar of thousands of cheering voices filled the night. Outside the window, John could see the nearby guard tower abandoned while the hundreds of prisoners silhouetted by the flames started pouring over the walls from Section Six. "Holy shit!" cried Steve, "It's a mass breakout!" Everybody was stunned at the epic spectacle that was unfolding before them. The roar of humanity battling for their freedom below was tremendous.

Suddenly, a half-dozen guards burst forth into the hospital ward. Their abrupt entry just about gave everyone a heart attack. The guards had terrified looks on their faces and started to yell frantically at the foreigners. They were tugging at their uniforms and pointing at the prisoners. It took a moment for John to realize what they wanted; they wanted everyone's spare prison garbs! "Quick! Everybody hand them your extra uniforms!" yelled John. The guards threw off their clothes, quickly changed into the prisoner uniforms and dashed back out as quickly as they came.

With two thousand prisoners all making a run for it, it was sheer chaos outside. The momentum of events was clear now; the guards were on the run and in a matter of minutes, the last barrier would be penetrated. John yelled out; "Okay, everyone grab your shit and be ready to run for it!" It was every man for himself now. John grabbed the cover off of his pillow and placed his few remaining possessions inside. He also grabbed a piece of paper lying on the table and stuffed it into his pocket. As they were ready to make their move, another guard dashed into the hospital ward. He screamed frantically "Everybody leave now! Go, Go, Go."

This was their cue to exit stage left. John and the others dashed out of the hospital wing and straight into the churning mass of desperate humanity outside. At that moment, the mob psychology was so intent on escape that virtually no one even noticed the presence of westerners among them. This was just fine with John; they just needed to blend in with the crowd and ride this train to freedom.

Beyond the main prison gate, numerous fire trucks were lined up waiting to come in but the guards had already fled. When the gates were finally opened, two thousand rioting prisoners rushed the gate in a mad dash for freedom. John and the others melted in with the stampeding mob and spilled outside the prison gates. In this already surreal scene, John saw Crazy Hassan furiously dragging his bed along to join the exodus. Once past the prison gates, John broke left and dashed through an open field and waded across a small river to reach the main highway. Dozens of passing trucks, busses and cars were already stopping to let prisoners clamber aboard. As the overloaded vehicles sped off down the road, John could see prisoners on the roof and sides clinging on for dear life.

John, Tom and Bernhardt managed to locate each other in the dim light but Pat had become separated and was nowhere to be found. They huddled in a shallow ditch to avoid being seen while they waited but it was almost impossible to find Pat in the dim light. Short of running around yelling out Pat's name, they weren't going to find him. John decided that they couldn't afford to hang around for Pat any longer without putting themselves at further risk. Their only hope now was to seek refuge at the American Consulate.

How to get to the consulate was a real dilemma. They could take their chances and commandeer a passing car but what if the driver decides to deliver them to the Revolutionaries instead? Most Iranians had been very good to them thus far, but now things were different in Iran; looking for Americans to hang seemed to be the new national mandate. The other option was to try to make it on foot, but it was quite a long distance to the consulate. None of them knew the city well enough to find it for sure. Besides, they sure as heck couldn't risk stopping and asking for directions. There was just too much unknown danger lurking everywhere. It was decided, they were going to have to take a risk and flag down a passing car.

"Here comes one" Tom whispered. "Okay, everybody on the road!" said John, and on that cue they flagged down the surprised motorist. They ordered the driver to take them to the American Consulate, but the astonished driver told them the American consulate had already been burned down. Burned to the ground or not, John told the driver to take them there anyway. They had to get away from there ASAP before they were spotted by any fanatics. John figured if the American consulate was really burned down, they could head for the Canadian consulate or the German Consulate.

In a moment of reality check, the driver hesitated a moment to look over the motley bunch standing in their prison garbs. It had probably crossed the driver's mind that this was certainly not a good night to be caught driving around with "devil" Americans in his car, but the driver's sense of humanity prevailed. "Okay get in, I take you there", he said.

Chapter 19

From the Fire into the Fry Pan

After driving at breakneck speeds through Tabriz, the trio safely reached the American consulate in one piece. Luckily there were no roadblocks and nobody took pot shots at them. In addition to all of their troubles, they were fugitives on the lam now. Then again, the real problem wasn't that they were running from the law; the problem was that there was no law. Lawless bands of armed gunmen would be their new worry, not the police. It was all getting pretty crazy.

John profusely thanked the anonymous driver before he sped off into the dark night. Everything was eerily quiet on Shah Naz Avenue where the consulate was located. The consulate appeared dark and possibly abandoned, but it wasn't burned down as they had been told. They yelled and banged on the gate hoping to arouse anyone still inside. Failing that, they were going to try to scale the walls to get inside. John just hoped none of the guards would be too trigger happy if it came to that. This was their only bastion of safety in this madness. They had to get inside before any of the really radical Islamists found them and made good on their threats. After a few minutes, an old man emerged out of the darkness and asked what they wanted. John informed him they were Americans in danger and they needed sanctuary right now! The old man nodded his head in acknowledgement of their plight and opened the gate to let them in. He told the unexpected guests to wait there by the gate while he fetched the Consul.

John was dying for a smoke, but he had left all of cigarettes behind. He felt around in the pillow case that he had stuffed with whatever was within an arms reach before he dashed out of the prison. Inside, he found he had a T-shirt, a towel, a spoon and a bar of soap, but no cigarettes. "Damn, what was I thinking?" muttered John.

A few minutes later, Michael Metrinko came out to the gate to welcome the wayward trio inside. "I've been watching the prison fire on TV. I was planning to come out and check up on you guys at first light." Michael grinned, "Thanks for saving me the trip out there. I wasn't too keen on leaving the compound with the shit that's going down everywhere."

"Yeah, ditto on that man." John echoed.

"Come on in and tell me about how the hell you guys busted out of jail" said Metrinko, laughing. "Looks like I'll be guilty of harboring fugitives!"

The quip helped to take a little edge off of their situation. For the moment, everyone felt a lot safer. The chaos, fear and uncertainty they had experienced at the prison was behind them for now. They walked through the darkened consulate compound towards Metrinko's residence. The compound was virtually deserted; it was just Metrinko and the old gate guard keeping watch now. Everyone else had either been evacuated or abandoned their posts.

After they dropped off their meager belongings at his residence, Metrinko offered to lead the trio over to the commissary and allowed them to help themselves to some food and drink. They also made a stop at the class VI store (liquors & spirits) to grab a few bottles of whisky and wine. Considering what they had gone through that day, and with no assurance of surviving tomorrow, getting plastered seemed like the thing to do.

****

John expected Pat and the other foreigners to be showing up at the consulate sometime during the night. John waited up into the early hours of the morning hoping to hear a knock at the gate, but the bottle of Jim Beam he, Tom and Bernhard had knocked out finally lulled him off to sleep.

When morning dawned on the 13th of February, there was still no sign of Pat or the others. John was beginning to worry about Pat; perhaps he and the others had not been as fortunate as they were. Maybe they ran into a lynch mob looking for American blood. Or perhaps they had been captured and were being held as hostage to extract demands from America. John was starting to get worried about his missing buddy.

About ten o'clock in the morning, Metrinko received a call from the local revolutionary committee (Khomitee') headquarters. They informed him that Pat and several of his fellow inmates were fine and safe and in their care. As it turned out, Pat's group had gone under the protection of Colonel Ibrahim, one of the political prisoners who had shared the hospital ward with them. Pat and the others felt that it was wise to stay close to him as he was a known leader of the revolutionaries. An odd choice, as the revolutionaries were the ones that professed the desire to kill Americans!

About a half hour later, a minibus pulled up in front of the consulate and Pat, Adolf, Ben and Steve got out. John gave his pal a big hug and said "Hell, I thought you were dead". Amazingly, everyone had made it out of prison without a scratch. Naturally, this joyous reunion called for even more bottles to be snitched from the Class VI store.

While everyone was busy retelling the details of their perspective of the great escape, Metrinko listened silently for the most part. He knew everyone had been through a lot of stress and the story telling was a cathartic release. There was the initial euphoria of having come through a life threatening event, but the celebration was short-lived as it quickly dawned on everyone that their safety at the consulate was at best, a very tenuous one. The reality was that the consulate was now under a virtual siege and communications to the outside was haphazard at best. Everybody was eager to make a hasty exit from Iran before things got any worse. As the U.S. counsel, everyone looked to Metrinko for guidance. John broke the question first. "So Mike, what's the drill to get us out of the country?"

Metrinko calmly patted his two German shepherds and gave a curt reply, "Who knows?"

He couldn't have said it better. Under the present circumstances, the truth was that he was just as trapped and helpless as the others. They were in the middle of a revolution and revolutions were a messy business. He knew things could quickly go from bad to worse. After all, this was largely a revolution about THEM. The hatred of America and its military and political presence in Iran were the catalysts that brought about this revolution. They couldn't simply walk out claiming neutrality. With all vestiges of protocol and legality in limbo now, they were entirely at the mercy of events that were well beyond their control. They would just have to wait and see.

****

Things outside quieted down over the next couple of days.

Other than an occasional crackle of gunfire in the distance, it seemed the worst was over. With idle time on their hands and nowhere to go, John and the others proceeded to make them selves at home in Metrinko's residence. They consumed prodigious amounts of alcohol and jammed to tunes from Metrinko's record collection. They killed time reading magazines, playing cards or playing with the dogs. Everybody was beginning to feel that in a few more days, order would be restored and they could seriously think about leaving the country.

Any feelings of improving security were cruelly dashed on the third day. Word came over the radio that the American Embassy in Tehran had been attacked and taken over by the revolutionary guards. Upon hearing the news, Metrinko became concerned that they might try to do the same thing to the Tabriz consulate. He asked John and his friends to go over to the consulate building and help him destroy communications equipment and burn documents. Before the day was out, word came over the radio that the revolutionary guards had released the embassy personnel in Tehran and had left the premises. This bit of news took the edge off the tension, but just how events would play out over the next few days was unknown. When they finally were done smashing the cipher and other communications gear, John and the others went back into Metrinko's residence to resume their pastimes.

Later that afternoon, the staccato of gunfire outside began to pick up again. From inside of the compound, the fighting seemed to be growing in intensity and moving closer. Occasionally, there was a loud but distant 'Boom' which was probably from tanks firing their main guns. So far the consulate had been left alone and that was a positive sign, especially after what had happened in Tehran. Everyone gathered around in Metrinko's living room and spoke in hushed tones now. There seemed to be an unspoken agreement to keep the chatter down so that one ear could constantly monitor the tempo and distance of the gunfire.

Some in the group began talking of leaving the compound and trying to make their own escape out of the country. Instead of feeling safe inside the consulate walls, they were beginning to feel like they were sitting ducks there. With civil order breaking down, they were sure the borders would not have the usual level of organized security. If they made it to the Turkish border, they figured they could just walk across a remote part of the border. John didn't think escape was such a hot idea. He figured they'd be caught long before they ever got to the border. If some trigger happy nut didn't do them in, getting lost out in the desert would. At least inside the consulate, they had enough food and drink to last them a good month or more. He thought it was still much too early to make such a radical move; it would be better to take a wait and see attitude.

Any talk of escape was abruptly cut short when the living room windows suddenly exploded in a deafening hail of gunfire. As bullet holes raced across the opposite wall, John instinctively dove to the floor and before he new it, he found himself down in the basement. Above them, an enormous volume of gunfire was still pouring into the room they had occupied moments before and a few of the ricocheting rounds found their way down to the basement. John and the others were certain they would be killed at any moment now. They were coming for them. John's heart was pounding, a million thoughts raced through his head. Who had been killed? Who was wounded? Would mom and dad ever know what happened to him? So is this how I am going to die?

Chapter 20

Escaping the Noose

Moments before the shooting had started, Metrinko had been working alone inside the main consulate building. Out of the corner of his eye, he saw movement where there shouldn't have been any. He looked out the window and saw a group of about 15 gunmen scaling the consulate walls. Alarmed by the sudden intrusion, he sensed things were quickly getting out of control. He picked up the phone and made an urgent call to some close contacts at the Revolutionary Khomitee' headquarters.

Speaking in fluent Farsi, Metrinko informed them that the consulate compound was under attack by their men and that they had better call them off now! They were attacking United States territory and violating international law! Khomitte' headquarters disavowed authorizing any such action against the consulate; these gunmen were probably renegade extremists operating on their own. With the sound of automatic weapons fire audible in the background, the commander of the Revolutionary guards told Metrinko to hold on. Help was on the way! Metrinko was a cool head, but this was rapidly becoming his worst nightmare. They had completely shot up his residence and he was certain some of his charges inside were already dead or wounded. He felt sick as he pleaded desperately on the phone, "You'd better also send me an ambulance; I think they've shot some of my people!"

Metrinko was still on the phone when the door burst open and three angry armed men rushed in and grabbed him. They pushed him flat back on his desk. The leader of the gunmen pointed his 9mm at Metrinko's head. "You are CIA spy. I put you under arrest." Meanwhile, one of the other gunmen grabbed the American flag off its pole and began tearing it into strips. Desperate to stall for time, Metrinko vehemently protested that what they were doing was an act of criminal aggression against the United States. He made it clear that the Khomitee' leadership would be very angry at what they were doing. If they harmed a U.S. diplomatic official, they would ultimately have to answer to the Ayatollah himself. Metrinko's protests fell on deaf ears. The leader threatened, "You are American CIA spy; you shut up!"

The other gunmen finished tying the remnants of the American flag into a crudely fashioned noose. They bound Metrinko's hands behind his back and placed the noose around his neck. With a nod from the leader, they dragged him outside to search for a good place to hang him. The end seemed imminent for Michael Metrinko as the gunmen found a nice strong tree in the courtyard from which to hang him. With a gleeful look, one threw the crude rope over the branch while another had brought along a chair with him. It seemed that it was all over for Metrinko now.

Thankfully, a loud commanding voice interrupted the lynching. "In the name of the Ayatollah and the Revolutionary Khomitee', you will stop this madness immediately!" Three Iranian Air force officers from the Revolutionary Khomitee' had arrived and not a moment too soon. The officers knew Metrinko personally and were furious at the gunmen's actions. They demanded to know who gave them the order to hang a diplomatic official of the U.S.?

As Metrinko stood ready to be hung, a heated debate erupted between the leader of the gunmen and the Air Force officers about whether Metrinko was a CIA spy or a bona fide diplomat. The Air Force officers insisted there was absolutely no proof that Metrinko was a spy and that such matters were way above their heads to pass judgment on. If they were wrong, they would be committing a serious international crime – and then they would have to answer to the Ayatollah with their own heads. Were they prepared for that?

At last some sense seemed to prevail with the hot-headed gunmen. After some more bickering, both sides reached agreement. They would formally arrest everyone inside the compound as anti-revolutionaries, but without conceding off-hand that they were CIA spies. They would take the Americans down to the Revolutionary Khomitee' headquarters where they would be judged and dealt with accordingly - by the senior Khomittee' members. The compromise at least placated the trigger-happy gunmen while it bought some temporary reprieve for the hapless Americans. With the situation now under control, one of the Air Force officers tended to Metrinko to see if he was alright. "I am very sorry, very sorry sir".

"I'm okay" said Metrinko, visibly shaken and rubbing his neck. He nodded toward his residence, "But I think they shot some of my people."

Chapter 21
The Nest of Spies

The shooting had stopped and John heard voices yelling upstairs. Everyone stayed put in the basement and said their final prayers. They were all frozen with fear and there was nowhere to run. The footsteps above them were amplified by the crunching of glass underfoot. Amazingly, no one had been killed or wounded despite the enormous volume of bullets that had penetrated the building. But did that matter? They would all be killed now.

The gunmen and the Air Force officers brought Metrinko back to his residence. When he saw his residence riddled with bullet holes, Metrinko immediately feared the worst. "Good God," muttered Metrinko.

John heard the voices and footsteps coming down into the basement. Two gunmen entered the basement and called out in excited voices to announce their discovery. They didn't shoot, but when John finally looked up, he saw the muzzle of gun pointed at his head. The men had a rather gleeful look on their on their faces. The gunman smiled at John and said "Aha! CIA spy!"

John and the others were rounded up and led out of the basement. One by one they emerged out of the basement with their hands up. Metrinko was relieved beyond words, moreover he was astonished that not one person had so much as a scratch on them! As the last person came out safe and sound, Metrinko could hardly contain his amazement. "This is a fucking miracle! By God, it is a fucking miracle!" he could hardly contain himself.

"Your dogs, they're okay too," said Steve, "I tried to get them to come out, but they're totally freaked out and wouldn't budge."

While everyone thanked their lucky stars that they were still alive, word had already gotten around town that a nest of CIA spies had been captured at the American consulate. Within minutes, an angry mob began to gather outside of the consulate walls and began chanting, *"Death to America, death to CIA!"* Metrinko muttered to himself, "Oh shit, now what?"

The Air Force officers called Khomitee' headquarters and arranged for transportation of the Americans. Shortly thereafter, a city bus pulled up in front of the compound to take Metrinko and the other nine detainees downtown. To show off their prize catch, the gunmen were allowed to triumphantly escort the group of prisoners towards the bus. As they neared the bus, the angry chanting grew more deafening. Fear gripped the group as the full fury and rage of an angry mob was vented at them at close range. This was the angry anti-American mobs that they had seen on TV. Only this time, it was up close and very personal.

Adolf took to his usual solace by reciting passages to himself from his book of Buddhist meditations. This caught the eye of one of the gunmen who apparently thought Adolf was reading from the bible. Clearly agitated by this affront to the Islamic revolution in progress, the gunman grabbed the book and tried to pry it out of Adolf's hands. Incredibly, the normally docile Adolf stubbornly refused to let go of his book and began struggling with the gunman! Surrounded by an angry mob and trigger-happy vigilantes, Adolf's sense of timing could not have been more abysmal.

Witnessing this supreme act of obstinate stupidity, John finally screamed at Adolf, "Goddammit Adolf! This is not the time! Give him the fucking book!"

The others looked on in shocked disbelief as Adolf, of all people, was now going to get them all killed over some lousy book! In the middle of this chaotic struggle, a shot rang out causing everyone to fall to the ground. The half-dozen trigger happy gunmen thinking they were being fired upon suddenly opened up in every direction with automatic weapons fire. They indiscriminately fired into nearby buildings and windows. This caused even more panic and mayhem and sent people scurrying for cover. John found himself under the bus, cursing Adolf's name.

Perhaps it was because the gunmen had all emptied their ammo clips that the shooting stopped as abruptly as it had begun. When it seemed safe, John crawled out from underneath the bus and dusted himself off. Everyone's nerves were frazzled again, but they were otherwise unhurt and the loading of the prisoners resumed. Adolf had been victorious in keeping his book and he held it close to his chest. John took one look at Adolf's blissful, self-righteous face and scowled "I ought to burn that fucking book my self, Adolf!"

This was already their second near death experience in a single afternoon. John wondered just how much longer their luck could hold out. They had to be running out of their quota of miracles.

Chapter 22
Brothers of the Revolution

As the bus pulled up to the Revolutionary Guard headquarters, there was yet another angry mob to greet them. The now familiar hateful chants filled the air to welcome the captured "spies." This time, their arrival was eagerly anticipated by a large group which included photographers and TV cameramen. As the Americans disembarked from the bus, the papparazi rushed forward to capture images of the alleged "CIA spies." Along with the flashing cameras and the chanting, raised fists were thrust in their faces as they were led into the Khomitee' headquarters. Inside the headquarters, it was no less a mad house. The whole building was packed wall-to-wall with people shoving and pushing, eager to be witness to the unfolding spectacle – and possibly some executions if they were lucky.

With the guards shoving their way past the mass of angry humanity, the Americans were marched into a large room and made to stand in front of the Revolutionary leaders and the Mullahs (clerics). Luckily, Michael Metrinko was immediately recognized by the senior leadership. Metrinko had performed his duties well as consul and had forged a close relationship with the Iranian leadership in Tabriz. He spoke fluent Farsi and over the years they had come to know him well as a man of integrity and honor. Despite the current ill sentiment towards America, Metrinko was still their honored guest and trusted friend. They held him in high esteem. The close relationships and good will he had banked would be needed more than ever on this day.

To the great dismay of the vigilantes and others who were hoping for a harsh reception, the Khomitee' leaders gave Michael a hearty welcome and apologized profusely for the rough treatment he had received from some of the overzealous revolutionaries. One of the Mullahs took this opportunity to severely chastise the vigilante gunmen for trying to hang a diplomatic official. "Allah has no place in paradise for those who take the lives of others whose guilt is unproven. Shame to all of you!" Having been cut down to size by the elders, the gunmen were sent away. The leaders then invited Metrinko to retire to a conference room for some tea and food where they could discuss a solution to the situation at hand.

****

While Metrinko and the Khomitee' leadership were off discussing the difficult issues of the moment, John and the others were still under suspect as hated spies. They were left lined up against a wall under the glare of TV cameras and lights. Nobody knew for sure who these foreigners were. Where had they come from? Why were they all hiding in the basement of the American consulate? One of the men, apparently a reporter, worked his way near the Americans and yelled "What are your names? What are your jobs at consulate?"

Everyone looked at each other unsure of whether they should even answer in the absence of Metrinko. John figured that this was Iran and they had no right to remain silent so somebody better say something quick. When nobody answered, the reporter then asked "Are you CIA spies?"

"Hell no!" John blurted out without even thinking. Now that he had spoken, he realized that he was the official spokesman for the group in the absence of Metrinko.

"Then, what are your jobs at the consulate?" probed the reporter again.

John wondered if he should have even opened his mouth now. This could all get out of hand even before Metrinko comes back. "What the hell…" thought John. Just standing there mute made them look guilty as hell anyhow.

"We're just tourists seeking shelter from the political troubles." John said just to throw them a bone to chew on. With that, the murmur in the room shot up a few notches.

One man shouted "Liar! CIA!", while another yelled "American spies!" They weren't buying this, thought John. And why would they? This was mob rule now, the truth didn't matter anymore. As far as everyone in the room was concerned, they surely must all be spies. There was simply no way they could talk themselves out of this one.

As if to remind the hapless prisoners that their lucky stars were fading fast, one of the guards then stepped forward. He pulled out his pistol and waved it menacingly in the faces of John and the others. He gleefully declared *"Spies! Aha! CIA! CIA!"…"You die now!"*

****

Outside the building the angry crowd was growing ever larger and the chanting louder. Hundreds were now attempting to force their way into the building, in hopes of getting a chance to curse and spit at the hated CIA spies inside. Every few minutes, the guard outside would fire his weapon to quell the surging mob. With every "kaboom" of the G2 rifle, everyone's heart skipped a beat. It appeared now that the end was really near for all of them. These people were solidly convinced they were CIA. Surely by dawn they would all be executed. If it came to that, John just hoped it would be over quickly.

In the room nearby, Metrinko expertly negotiated at length with the Khomitee' leadership. Metrinko could hear the chanting and the gunfire and he knew that time was running short. He had to get John and the others out of immediate danger. The momentum of the events was so powerful that the Khomitee' leadership itself could totally lose control of the situation. With radical gunmen on the loose and a hostile mob building outside, Metrinko knew that he had little time to defuse an extremely volatile situation.

Metrinko diplomatically told the Khomitee' leadership that there has been an unfortunate mistake; the foreigners with him are not CIA at all. In fact several of them were Europeans, not Americans. The members of leadership listened with concern and pondered the volatile situation. They did not doubt Metrinko's word as a man of honor, but the leadership was in a serious political quandary now. They acknowledged that perhaps an embarrassing mistake had been made, but the leadership would lose serious face if they simply apologized and released the Americans outright. After all, the revolution looked to the Khomitee's leadership to overthrow the Shah and bring America to her knees. Thousands outside were demanding execution for the "spies." They had to put on a show of just strength to the public.

Metrinko suggested that they should conduct a public hearing. The TV cameras were already there and the senior leadership could question the foreigners publicly to determine their true status. This way the leadership could save face by appearing to be in control of the situation and meting out appropriate justice to the accused. Metrinko gambled that this was the lesser of two evils. At worst, his charges would be sent back to prison and that was a far sight better option than the jeopardy they were in now.

****

Although the thought of going back to jail wasn't appealing, John was damned if he was going be shot as CIA spy. He'd happily trade a few more years in prison over being dead for all the wrong reasons. He had mulled over his options and he decided he had to come clean about his status as an escapee from jail if he were to live another day.

After what had seemed like an eternity, Metrinko and the senior Khomitee' leadership re-entered the room. The sight of Metrinko walking in was a welcome relief to everybody. For a while, it had seemed that they would all meet their demise either from the angry mob outside, a trigger-happy guard or by firing squad. The five senior members of the Khomitee' leadership sat down across from the accused. One of them raised his arms and waited for the room to quiet down.

"We the Khomitee' leadership, have decided to determine the true identity of these nine men who stand before you today. These men have been brought here, accused of being American CIA spies. If that is proven to be true, they will be dealt with harshly as such criminals. However, if they are found to be innocent of the charges, they will be justly treated as the Quran demands."

John couldn't understand what was being said, but he could sense that there was now some semblance of order and justice where minutes before there was none. Metrinko stood in silence near the foreigners. He had done for his flock what he could. He had leveraged his remaining power and influence discreetly in private. Now, back in the public eye, this was no longer his place to speak out. It was up to each of the nine men to somehow prove their innocence.

The senior leader of the revolutionary Khomittee' stood up to speak. "The American Consul, Mr. Metrinko is an honored friend of mine. Not all Americans are evil, he is a good man. He swears on his honor that these men are not CIA. If this is true, then the accused must now reveal to us truthfully, who they are and what is the nature of their business here." He then nodded to Metrinko to translate what he had just said.

The moment of truth had come for everyone. As if by unspoken agreement, everyone turned again to John to speak for the group. Their next stop may be prison once again, but they had no choice but to let truth take its course. John faced the leadership and spoke "Sir, all of us here…we are escaped prisoners from jail, sir".

The totally unexpected response stirred up the packed room into frenzy. It took a minute for the room to calm down again.

"Escaped from jail you say? All of you?"

"That is right sir. We were held in Tabriz Prison for the past seven months. We escaped several days ago during the prison fire and mass breakout." John wiped the sweat from his forehead. "We ran for our own safety like everyone else. We went to the American consulate only to seek safe refuge."

The buzz in the room exploded with amazement and excitement at the unexpected turn of events. The hearing was suddenly taking on a whole new life of its own. It was a real time drama in the making. It seemed all of Tabriz was now glued to their

TV sets.

"Will you please tell us, why were you put in jail, under what charges?"

John cleared his throat "We were hired as drivers by a Pakistani businessman named Abdullah". John figured that mentioning a Foreigner as the bad guy was good move here. "He told us that he ran an auto import business and he needed drivers to bring the cars to Iran. But this man Abdullah, he turned out to be a smuggler. He also altered our passports so when we tried to leave, we were arrested at the border for customs and passport violations. We were deceived by this man and put in jail while he is still free." That came out well, thought John.

By now the anticipation in the room was electrifying. The crowd hung on every word as it was translated into Farsi. The man in charge listened to John's story with empathy. More than likely, John and the others weren't completely ignorant of their acts as they claimed. On the other hand, these men were clearly not the spies they were looking for either.

"This is a very interesting story, but how can you prove this? How can we even believe that you were really in prison?"

"That's the truth sir...I don't know what else to tell you." John didn't know what else to say. They all stood there and looked at each other for answers as helpless people often do. How could they prove anything at all? They had lost everything they had. They would need to find witnesses or some indisputable evidence, but how? It was not as if they would be assigned lawyers and given time to gather evidence for a case presentation. It was now, or never. There would likely be no second chances.

Suddenly John understood a mysterious impulse that night of the prison breakout. None of it made any sense then and he gave little thought to it since, but now it was all clear to him. Before he fled prison, John inexplicably grabbed a piece of paper nearby and placed it in his pocket. At the time, he didn't even know what it was he had grabbed. It was all reflexive and he didn't even remember consciously doing it. Since that night, he had pulled it out of his pocket a few times forgetting it was even there. At one point, he even thought of throwing it away, but something made him put it back each time. The sudden realization that this was no mere coincidence sent a chill down his spine. He again reached into his pocket and pulled out the ragged piece of paper. It was not a figment of his imagination. It was still there by God! Tattered but it was really there. Until this very moment it held almost no other significance, but now it was a ticket that could now spare their lives. His hand shook a bit as he held out the little shred of paper.

"This…is the receipt for my clothes and personal items when I was processed in at the prison." John said, still in disbelief at what had just happened. The others looked at John in astonishment while this development sent the room into another tizzy. Nobody could have scripted this. The drama was all too compelling.

A guard took the paper and handed it to the speaker. He examined it closely, nodded his head and passed the piece of paper around to the other Khomitee' members. They each nodded in agreement that these men really must have been held in prison. The proof was indisputable. These men were not spies.

The Khomitee' now had an embarrassing little problem of their own: The arrival of the captured "spies" had been televised as the big news of the day. They would now have to admit these were not CIA spies, but simply doing that would make them lose face politically. They now had to do damage control and figure out how to "explain" these foreigners to an angry public with a positive spin.

The man that had been questioning them was obviously a politically astute man. He seemed to know just what to do.

"Tell me, have you all been tried and received sentences for your accused crimes?" He asked.

"No sir" said John. "Actually, none of us have gone to trial yet. With the revolution and all, our trials kept getting delayed again and again."

"I understand" said the man. "So we have determined that you are not spies, but we must still determine your guilt or innocence of the charges that put you in jail in the first place. The Khomitte' will now investigate the facts of the case and return with a judgment after lunch".

****

It was yet another miracle; they had dodged the bullet once again. The foreigners were taken to a nearby room down the hall where they were questioned and their statements taken. This was already John's third iteration of having to state his case so it was merely a matter of formalities. Rumor was that the Ministry of Justice building had been attacked and ransacked so more than likely, their original case files had been lost or destroyed by now.

After the statements had all been taken down, lunch was brought in for everyone. They were told to enjoy their lunch while the judges ate their meals and deliberated their fate down the hall. Knowing they were no longer considered spies and candidates for execution seemed to have brought out everyone's appetite. Confession never felt so good. The meal seemed especially tasty and satisfying after living off of Oreos and beef jerky for days. Above all, John realized how dehydrated he was and gulped down several bottles of soda in rapid succession.

After the harrowing ordeal they had just gone through, the prospect of returning to prison wasn't so bad after all. At least everyone knew they would be safer there. After they had rested for about an hour, everyone was led back into the "courtroom". The man who had questioned them earlier entered, and the room went silent. The whole city waited with baited breath for their verdict. For John and his friends, this was their third moment of truth in the course of single day.

The man smiled and pronounced in a tone perhaps too nonchalant for such a crucial moment. "We the leaders of the Khomitee' have reviewed the situation of your imprisonment at Tabriz prison. We are all in agreement that you have been unfairly imprisoned under the cruel and unjust laws of the Shah. We deem it unjust that you were jailed while the real criminals have gone free. Therefore, as victims of the corrupt policies under the Shah, you are declared innocent of all charges. You are all free to go!"

John and the others could not believe their ears. They hugged each other and rejoiced in their acquittal. No more jail, no death by firing squad! An hour or two ago they were preparing to die in front of a firing squad, and now they were free to go. The mood in the courtroom had radically shifted from anger and hatred to jubilation in the course of an afternoon. One anonymous man stepped forward and declared out loud for all the world to hear, "You have been oppressed by the Shah! You are brothers of the revolution!" and proceeded to give John a big hug. The gallery went wild and all of Tabriz celebrated their new brothers of the revolution that day.

Chapter 23
The Long Road Home

It had been a most amazing turn of events wrapped into a single incredible day. Yet, as wonderful as their verdict was, everyone's jubilation was short-lived and tempered by the reality of the situation. They were still stuck in the middle of a violent revolution in a country where millions of angry people still wanted them dead. They had no passports, no money and no means of getting home. Their freedom was regained, but in the reality of the situation, it sure didn't count for much. Getting home safely was about as easy as going to Mars.

The chaotic series of events that day demonstrated that the power and control exerted by the local Khomitee' over the city's armed revolutionaries was tenuous at best. Beyond the city of Tabriz, the local Khomitee' simply had no power and no control. By their own admission, they did not even know exactly what the situation was in other cities across Iran. Who knew what anarchy existed out there? Under these chaotic and dangerous circumstances, providing reliable and safe passage to Tehran was simply out of the question. After discussions with Metrinko, the Khomitee' leaders decided to send the foreigners back to the American Consulate until the situation stabilized and a viable solution could be found.

Until the storm of revolution played itself out around them, the consulate walls would provide a modicum of safety.

****

Back at the consulate, everything was back to square one. Even after all that they had endured that day they were for all intents and purposes, under siege again. Although the Khomittee' leaders generously posted a couple of guards outside the compound walls, it was still too unsafe to venture outside. The sounds of periodic firefights announced in no uncertain terms that the revolution was still being openly contested by forces still loyal to the Shah. Add to that, radical vigilantes and renegade groups not firmly under the control of the Khomitee' were still a potential wild card.

Caution and prudence became the order of the day. After what had happened, no one took anything lightly anymore. The shattered windows and bullet holes were a reminder of the serious danger that could revisit them at any time. They now exercised caution even when moving between buildings within the compound. There was always a slim chance that some rogue sniper could take a pot shot at them. They had all faced down certain death once too many times in the past few days and nobody wanted to take any unnecessary chances. They all knew they were still living on borrowed time as long as they were trapped in Iran.

A nervous sort of boredom began to creep in as the days passed. One morning, John was awakened by nearby gunfire. Still groggy from sleep and a bit hung over, he kept one eye open and an ear to the ground. This time he heard something different. A rumbling noise was approaching the compound from the east. As the noise grew louder the ground began to tremble. John suddenly recognized the source of the noise. He had heard it before when Army convoys used to pass through town during the annual military exercises in

Germany. A rush of adrenaline shook him out of his grogginess as he shot upstairs to the balcony window. Looking beyond the compound walls, he could see it was a tank approaching along a side street. John recognized the tank as a British-built Chieftain tank. Armed with a powerful 120-millimeter canon, its firepower was about equivalent of that of a 5-inch shell fired from a Navy destroyer.

John hesitated a moment to alert the others thinking perhaps it would just pass them by. That bit of wishful thinking was cast aside as the tank stopped directly across from his position. Several others had been awakened by the commotion outside and had come upstairs to join John. They all stood spellbound as the turret of the tank began to turn towards them. If the compound were its intended target, they were most certainly finished.

They watched with dumbfounded relief as the big gun swung past them and towards another building across the street. Suddenly, a bright yellow flash lit up the entire block but it was the blast and shockwave a split second later that snapped everyone out of their stupor. Almost in unison, a chorus of *"Holy Shit!"* rang out from the group as the building across the street exploded in flame and dust. The natural urge was to run and get the hell out of there before the tank commander turned the gun on them next. Yet, there was no place to run, no place to hide from this. John and the others could only watch with a fatalistic detachment as what could be their last impressions of life unfolded before them. After what seemed to be an eternity, the tank starting moving back down the street and the sound slowly faded away as the group sat in silence staring out the broken windows. Once again, luck had smiled on them, but how much longer would it last? They had been two weeks inside the cauldron of the Iranian revolution and so far, everyone in the group was unscathed. Still, getting out of Iran alive seemed a mission impossible.

****

As the ensuing days dragged on, Metrinko was busily negotiating with the revolutionary guard Khomitee' to obtain safe passage for the consulate refugees. In spite of the on-going chaos in Iran, Metrinko had somehow managed to talk the Khomitee' into securing an Iranian Air Force C-130 to fly them out to Tehran. They wouldn't be out of the woods there, but just getting to the American Embassy in Tehran would be a big first step towards getting home.

First, Metrinko had a little bit of his personal business to take care of. In a quirk of personal priorities, Metrinko had been busy trying to figure out how to protect his personal belongings from the looting that would surely follow their departure from the consulate compound. Metrinko had decided that before they left the premises, he would leverage the refugees in his fold to help him inventory and move all of his precious belongings into the basement safe. It took John and his friends several hours, but they finally managed to move all of Metrinko's belongings into safekeeping. When it was all finally done, John sarcastically remarked, "Hey Metrinko, can we go home now?" Metrinko, not to be outdone responded "yeah, you'd better start packing your steamer trunks now" in an obvious jibe to the fact that everyone else had little more than the shirts on their backs.

****

Early the next morning, the Khomitee' came through as promised. A city bus pulled up to the gates to evacuate the foreigners. John and his friends had been ready since first light. They had gathered up what little belongings they had and waited anxiously to leave. Outside the compound, things were quiet but tensions ran high. In this uncertain environment, anything could happen to upset their plans. They swiftly and quietly clambered aboard the bus escorted by fifteen armed guards and departed for the local airbase. As they reached the first checkpoint, they wondered if there would be any trouble. What if some radical elements found out about their evacuation and they objected to letting the foreigners leave? Many of the most radical elements were still firmly clinging to the belief that the foreigners were all CIA spies. Thankfully, the Khomitee' was in charge at this checkpoint and they were allowed to pass without incident.

When they arrived at Tabriz Airbase, the escorting guards quickly clambered out and fanned out around the bus. A few of the guards moved cautiously ahead into the terminal building to make sure the coast was clear. When the signal was given, John and his friends were rushed into the waiting room and told to wait while the plane was readied for their flight. Tension filled the air in the waiting room as they were made to wait and wait. An hour passed, then two. "What the hell is the hold up?" muttered John.

At last, the group was finally herded onto the bus again and driven out to the plane waiting at the end of the runway. The engines were already running as its controversial human cargo scurried aboard and took their seats on the web netting. No sooner as the cargo door was closed, the plane began its takeoff roll. Seconds later the plane lifted off and headed for Tehran. A sense of relief engulfed everyone. After months of imprisonment and weeks of facing chaos and sudden death, they were at last taking their first tangible step towards what was hopefully freedom and home.

John and the others aboard were well aware that the situation in Tehran was largely unpredictable. For all they knew they could be simply be escaping one noose for another. Tabriz may have been the frying pan, but Tehran could be the fire that finally seals their doom. In just about an hour and a half, they would learn what fate holds for them in Tehran.

Tehran

At Tehran's international airport, everyone was herded off the C-130 and hastily taken into a holding area in the terminal. The Iranian authorities in Tehran were surprised to see foreigners, including Americans, arriving aboard the Iranian Air Force transport. Two guards who had escorted them from Tabriz tried to explain the rather unusual disposition of the new arrivals, but the lack of documentation only confused the issue. Except for Metrinko, no one else had passports or any form of identification. After some haggling by Metrinko, the authorities agreed to transport the foreigners to the American Embassy. They were happy to get the mystery guests off of their hands.

Like the consulate in Tabriz, the American Embassy in Tehran had been under virtual siege for the past several weeks. The radical Islamists were practically camped out outside the gates and any comings and goings from the embassy quickly brought out angry protesters swarming around vehicles like angry hornets. In order to expedite the transport of the group to the embassy, the airport authorities decided to pack them all into an ambulance and send them on their way with sirens wailing. The ruse worked well as the ambulance was allowed to enter the embassy compound largely unmolested by the crowd outside.

Inside the embassy walls, a well ordered chaos permeated the entire compound. Hundreds of people were streaming to the embassy daily seeking refuge and evacuation: American civilians, their families, Iranian employees who worked for the American companies. Over on one side, several officials were busy burning documents while others had set up tables to hastily process the hundreds of people waiting to be evacuated.

John and the others were disgorged from the ambulance and wandered into the fray. There were people milling around everywhere. They were going in every which direction, with people and luggage on the ground all around. At the center of all this commotion stood Colonel Leland Holland in full battle dress barking out instructions and directing the confused, milling masses toward the proper lines for processing. Metrinko gathered up his herd and reported to Colonel Holland. He informed Holland that he and his group had just come from Tabriz under trying circumstances. He wanted to make sure that everyone got new passports and a ticket home. In light of the situation, it seemed a tall order, but Colonel Holland quickly directed them over to the line where new passports were being issued on the fly.

Metrinko's services were badly needed here; the embassy staff was already overloaded and undermanned. Metrinko told his flock that he had to go now and that they would be in good hands from here on. They had all been through a lot together in these past couple of weeks. Everybody in the group thanked Metrinko for his heroic efforts and getting them to Tehran safely under these difficult conditions. Metrinko told them "Good luck and don't get anymore crazy ideas about driving cars to Iran." and then disappeared into the crowd. Everyone put on a stoic face, but more than a few eyes were misty.

****

"We'd better be going" said John. "It's going to take a while – we're not home yet". The group wandered over to join the mile-long line in the courtyard. While waiting in line, John wondered how the U.S. embassy could possibly issue passports to the non-U.S. nationals in the group. Maybe Bernhard, Adolf and Ben would be sent to their respective embassies. They would just have to see. While pondering their plight, it dawned on John; how could he himself possibly get a new passport issued without any proof of citizenship, or for that matter without any shred of identification? This was going to be interesting.

Eventually, he reached the head of the line and the passport officer asked John for his old passport or ID. With nothing to lose, John explained to the officer that his passport had been burned in the prison fire in Tabriz – along with any and all of his identification. "For that matter, he said, the next nine guys in line will tell you the same thing." John figured that this must have sounded like a pretty far-fetched story to the officer. It was sure to arouse skepticism and some questions. He was wondering if he might need to have them page Metrinko to corroborate their story. Much to John's surprise, the passport officer replied "Okay, No problem!" After taking down some basic information, he directed John to stand against the wall and snapped a quick Polaroid picture. On the table next to him were stacks of memo pads made from old government forms. In fact these were nothing more than outdated miscellaneous 8-1/2 by 11 government forms cut into quarters, then crudely bound along one edge with heavy glue.

To John's utter astonishment, the passport officer peeled off about a dozen sheets from one of the memo pads, taped the

Polaroid photo onto it, pressed the seal of the United States onto the front page and promptly signed it for good measure. The passport officer casually handed the pad over to John and said, "Here's your passport," good luck. John hesitated as he pondered the pathetic looking pad of paper in utter disbelief. Inside of the so-called passport were only blank pages – no entry stamps, nothing. No one was ever going to believe – not even for a second that this was a valid U.S. passport. Suddenly, the high hopes he had had just minutes before seemed to fade away. It was all so ludicrous, and utterly bizarre! This must be some kind of cruel joke; surely any moment now the passport officer is going to tap him on the shoulder and say, "Just kidding, here's your real passport." But this was no joke. In his hands was his only hope of getting out of Iran.

Next they all headed over to the evacuation line. After another long wait in the hot sun, they received their evacuation orders and plane tickets. The buses were constantly coming and going all day but they were still a good dozen busses away before their number would come up. When all of the travel arrangements had been arranged, they lined up again for some food and water. Everybody was thirsty and hungry but getting their evacuation papers in order had been of primary importance until now.

They found a little shaded area and finally sat down on the ground to eat and rest. Everyone was dead tired and few words were spoken. John and Pat lit up their smokes and sat quietly. No one talked about what they would do when they got out. It seemed nobody wanted to jinx their evacuation by getting cocky now. They had learned too well in recent weeks that you're not safe until you're really safe. Now it was "hurry up and wait" as John dozed off in the afternoon heat.

****

Late that afternoon, their number was finally called. John and Pat dusted themselves off and boarded their assigned evacuation bus. Many of the other passengers boarded with great trepidation. Understandably, leaving the sanctuary of the embassy walls was especially scary to some Iranians who were seeking political asylum in the U.S. Surely some of them had been involved with intelligence gathering and other sensitive activities which made them "agents of the Shah". In other words, prime candidates for arrest and probably execution.

Nervous tension filled the air as the bus departed the embassy. The violent protests of the past weeks were frightening enough as the busload of Americans and Westerners were now a concentrated and a highly public target. It seemed to take forever to get through the streets of Tehran and onto the expressway which led to the airport. They felt vulnerable and terribly exposed the whole way. The leering looks from some people on the street, together with the threatening graffiti everywhere, did nothing to alleviate the discomfort. Thankfully, the journey to the airport was uneventful but anything could still happen while they were still on hostile territory.

The airport was an absolute zoo as John joined the tens of thousands of frightened evacuees who were at risk from the new regime. They stepped off of the bus and were herded into the long line of evacuees that moved at a snail's pace. Most of the time, the line barely moved so most people just sat down on the ground. John could see there were a couple of revolutionary guards going down the line randomly checking passports. Rumor had it that they were looking for Savak agents trying to flee the country. "Oh crap", thought John. "They're going to want a word with me when they see my shitty passport." The two gunmen came by and looked at John, but they just kept on walking. It was a close one.

When the gunmen were about 10 meters down the line, John heard a commotion erupt. They had pulled a man out of line and his family was crying and begging for his release. It was a frightening thing to witness as they led him away at gunpoint. Over the next two hours, they came by again and again; about every twenty minutes. Each time, they looked at John with their steely eyes, but did not stop.

At last John reached the check-in counter. He had nothing to check as his "luggage" consisted of a dirty pillow cover containing a couple of pieces of borrowed clothing and a bar of soap – his sole remaining possessions. He traded in his ticket for a boarding pass and headed toward the gate.

The next hurdle would be the passport control. Two long lines slowly snaked their way to the checkpoint. John chose the left line and looked ahead to see how things were progressing. A couple of people with one of the makeshift passports seemed to be having trouble convincing the passport agents that they were legitimate. Sensing potential trouble, John instinctively slipped over to the right line. Perhaps the agent on this line would be a little less vigilant and not challenge him.

John's moment of truth arrived. He handed over his pathetic excuse of a passport over to the agent fully expecting its validity to be questioned. He had come this far against all odds, would this be the final hurdle that dooms him back to square one? It could just as easily be from here straight back to prison – perhaps even on new charges. Under the present circumstances, the acquittal in Tabriz meant little or nothing here. He kept cool and calm on the outside, but John knew very well that this could be the end of his amazing run of luck. The inspector checked his photo and flipped through the blank pages, John could only watch with detached numbness. Then, as if nothing were out of the ordinary, the officer stamped the passport and handed it back to John. He must have walked a dozen steps before he finally exhaled in relief.

As he wandered through the crowded terminal to find a open spot to sit down, everything was beginning to seem unreal as he sat waiting for the call to board his flight. Things seemed to be working in slow motion now. It was as if everything were a dream and that if he woke up, the miraculous events that had seen him through thus far would be wiped away by a much harsher reality. A strange Karma had enveloped him and it seemed any sudden moves now would upset the masterful equilibrium. He would just go with the flow until they were truly in safe territory again.

****

Another couple of hours passed before it was their turn to board the next evacuation flight. Everyone seemed to share in the unspoken need to stay calm and orderly. The boarding proceeded smoothly as the passengers quickly took to their seats on the Pan Am 747. There was no idle chatter to be heard in the cabin. Aside from a few hushed remarks, little was spoken amongst the passengers. Almost five hundred tense faces filled the cabin and everyone was eager to go. The crew was also eager to get going and went about busily securing the cabin for departure. It seemed everything was proceeding smoothly towards a timely departure when two armed men of the revolutionary guards boarded the aircraft. In an instant, the dreamlike state of the past couple hours was now shattered by a quiet murmur of angst spreading throughout the cabin. The gunmen went from passenger to passenger down each aisle demanding to see their passports. Slowly they began working their way towards the back of the plane where John was seated.

"Damn it! Not again!" he thought to himself. This time a cold chill swept through John. These men looked serious and unpredictable; much like those who had stormed the consulate. Amazingly, Pat just sat quietly staring ahead, almost as if he were frozen. Perhaps he had finally learned to control his body language; John was grateful for that. As the gunmen slowly made their way aft towards him, John could envision himself getting dragged off the plane at gunpoint - just like that hapless fellow a while back. If they dragged him off the plane now, he wished they would just shoot him to get it over with.

There he was, just minutes away from his final dash to freedom and now this again! The cruel irony of it all was too painful to contemplate. The gunman working his side of the plane was just two rows away now. John took one last look at his "Passport" and took a deep breath as he fully expected to be snagged in this final dragnet. Would it be like it was at Razi again? A momentary brush with freedom and then only to have it cruelly taken away? Even if John had nine lives, he had surely spent them all. As the gunman began to work the row in front of him, everything once again slowed down to a dreamlike state. Everything seemed to go silent and moved in fluid motions until suddenly, a loud voice speaking in Farsi rudely snapped John out of his trance.

It was the gunman on the other side; he had already finished his aisle. He was yelling and gesturing at his slower comrade that they had to leave now! Apparently, word had come over his radio that a second plane was already about to leave before it was searched. The gunman in front of John paused for a moment, unsure if he should still search the last few rows of seats. He then abruptly turned away and headed toward the front of the plane.

If John had never believed in miracles before, he had experienced yet one last miracle in a truly astonishing chain of events. As the gunmen disembarked and the doors closed, a collective sigh of relief swept through the plane. John nudged Pat and told him "Okay, you can breathe now". Pat closed his eyes and exhaled with relief "ohhhh….shit…." As soon as the stairs were cleared, the crew wasted no time in getting underway. The whine of the engines spinning up was like music to their ears.

In the waning light of the evening, the giant 747's wheels left the ground and the plane climbed westward towards Frankfurt, Germany. John Burchill, the wayward college dropout was finally going home at last. The carefree young man of the previous summer was now a bit wiser in the ways of the world. Liberty and life really meant something now that he had lost the first and come so very close to losing the latter. John knew he was damn lucky to have come out of it at all - still alive and in one piece. He had had his fill of adventure to last a lifetime. He was ready to go home.

When the pilot announced that they had finally cleared Iranian airspace, a chorus of wild cheering and whistles erupted in the cabin. It seemed that the entire cabin had held their breath until that moment. The bar was opened on the upper deck and the booze flowed freely. By the time they landed in Frankfurt some five hours later, not a drop was left aboard.

****

That day, February 27th, 1979, the embassy in Tehran had sent us a telegram notifying us that John was registered and processed for evacuation. It was the first time in many days that we were sure of his whereabouts and safety. We were also greatly relieved as that night on the evening news, we learned that the consulate in Tabriz had been ransacked and burned.

We were all elated at the wonderful news, but as yet we weren't sure when John would be getting home. The evacuation flights weren't on any published schedule and exactly which flight John would actually make it onto was another unknown. We would only know for sure when he had arrived safely in Germany. Until then, we could only wait in hopeful anticipation. We were prepared for an all night vigil when the phone rang around 10 pm; it was John! He was calling from the Frankfurt airport letting us know that he was okay. A great wave of relief swept over us as we hugged each other. Mom burst into tears at the news and kept thanking God that her prayers were answered. John was back in safe territory.

Dad told John to stay put - he would drive down to the airport to pick him up, but John refused the offer. He said he would really rather take the train home. He and Pat had decided that they had both been enough of a liability; they wanted the satisfaction of making it all the way home on their own. Dad understood; it was one small gesture by John to atone for his reckless actions. Dad told him to hurry home - we would all be waiting for him.

****

The airport connector train took John and Pat to Frankfurt's main train station where they would board separate trains for the final leg home. At that late hour, Frankfurt's cavernous Hauptbahnhof was nearly empty in the cold winter night. Their long and difficult ordeal together was finally over. Their little adventure of the previous summer had brought far more grief and pain to their families than they ever imagined. Now they would both have to go home and face their parents shortly. Perhaps being alone with their thoughts for the final hour or so would be helpful to "decompress" back to normal life. John was looking at a second chance at getting his life together. There was much to contemplate, and much to atone for.

Together, they walked slowly over to Track 9 where John's train would be departing for Butzbach. They were both exhausted by the physical and emotional toll of the past days and weeks. As they stood on the platform, their parting words were few and curt.

"Well, this is it Pat" said, John.

"Yeah, this is it." echoed Pat.

John gave Pat a big hug. "We're so damned lucky to be alive you jerk!"

"Yeah, enough of that shit already!"

"Take care of yourself, man."

"All right brother."

The conductor's whistle pierced the night. "I'd better go" said John as he turned and climbed aboard. As the train slowly pulled away, John waved and yelled to his friend "Hey, when I get home, I'll drink a beer to your return".

"And I'll drink double that to yours" retorted Pat as he watched John's train glide away into the night.

****

It was a freezing cold night in late February 1979 when John finally came home. A light snow was falling as the Cab drove away into the night. The wayward brother I thought I would never see again stepped out of the darkness. He was almost unrecognizable; he had lost over sixty pounds and looked gaunt and frail, his long hair had been cropped to a prison crew cut, and his once pale skin was now tanned and dark. We all embraced and welcomed this familiar stranger back home. He had beaten incredible odds to make it home safe and sound. It must have already been around two o'clock in the morning, but no sooner did my mother wipe away her tears did she dutifully set out a hot meal for John.

Afterword:

Two Years Later…

After returning from Iran, John straightened out his life and foreswore any more outlandish adventures. He had learned some hard lessons and took life a bit more seriously now. He even followed in dad's footsteps and took a job with the Army and Air Force Exchange Service. John worked hard, and steadily worked his way up to Base Exchange manager. A couple of years later, John moved to Comiso, on the island of Sicily to run the exchange operations there. The working life was predictable and routine, but his wanderlust for adventure was pretty much satiated.

Despite all that they went through together, John and Pat quickly drifted apart in the ensuing years. The last John had heard of Pat, he had gotten some German Fraulein pregnant and was driving a forklift for a company in Kaiserlautern. It seemed that they were now taking very separate paths in life.

One day, John's phone rang. It was Pat; "Hey John! How are ya! Look, I got this great deal driving cars to Syria! You want in?"

ISBN 141207269-7

Made in the USA